# I'd Rather Be Hunting

### STEPHEN W. SORENSON

HARVEST HOUSE PUBLISHERS
EUGENE, OREGON

**I'D RATHER BE HUNTING**
Copyright © 2014 by Stephen W. Sorenson
Published by Harvest House Publishers
Eugene, Oregon 97402
www.HarvestHousePublishers.com

Library of Congress Cataloging-in-Publication Data
  Sorenson, Stephen.
  I'd rather be hunting / Stephen W. Sorenson.
    pages cm
  ISBN 978-0-7369-5310-8 (pbk.)
  ISBN 978-0-7369-5311-5 (eBook)
  1. Hunting—Religious aspects—Christianity. I. Title.
  BV4597.4.S67 2014
  248.8'8—dc23
                                                      2013018012

---

*To my father, who graciously allowed me to
buy my first rifle when I was 13.*

*To my hunting friends, especially Roy (my father-in-law) and Walt,
who have shared so many adventures with me and positively
influenced my life more than they'll ever know.*

*To Amanda, my dear wife and hunting companion,
who has always known how much I need hunting adventures
in my life. She played such a key role in making this book happen.*

*And to Caitlin, for her encouragement,
laughter, and godly character.*

---

# Acknowledgments

Many people have made this book possible; and I'd like to thank some of them right now:

*Amanda*—wife, friend, hunter—often you anchor things at home so I can go hunting. The food and menus you provide to try to keep us eating the right stuff during hunting camp, which works most of the time, enable us to keep going no matter how bad hunting conditions become. And when I return, your great game meals motivate me to keep adding meat to the freezer. God uses you to bless me in so many ways. Thanks for hanging with me during this journey called life.

*Caitlin,* please forgive me for the time I spent hanging up that deer instead of fishing with you. It won't happen again. I love you.

*Steve Chapman,* thanks for the opportunity to follow your big shoes.

*Barbara Gordon,* not only are you a great editor, you are a joy to work with even though you insist (rightly, I might add) that I call "antelope" *pronghorn.* I appreciate the laughter we share. And, of course, a big thank you to *Terry Glaspey* and the rest of *the folks at Harvest House.*

*Roy and Walt,* you weave in and out of these stories. Thanks for believing in me and sharing life with me for more than 30 years. Words can't express how special you guys are to me. I'll never forget many of God's truths you actively live out.

*Blane,* you are a relatively new hunting buddy, and your enthusiasm and kindness mean a lot. I'll never forget how you patiently pulled more than 100 painful cactus spines out of my back after I rolled under that fence wearing two fleece jackets during elk hunting season. And Mike, your hunting excitement is contagious.

*Friends who have contributed stories and illustrations to this book*—you are generous and an inspiration. I wish I had more space on this page to list you by name!

*John,* your photography skills are amazing. You go above and beyond to assist me in communicating the adventure of hunting.

*Readers,* I know I may not be privileged to meet many of you in person but I thank you for reading these stories. It is indeed a privilege to share them with you. I hope you enjoy them.

# Contents

# My First Deer Hunt

I started hunting rabbits, woodchucks, and pheasants during my early teens in the Midwest.

I started hunting big game when I was 25.

Nobody in my immediate family had ever hunted; I was the first. In fact, I learned several years ago that my aunt and uncle had given away rifles and shotguns they inherited because they didn't know anybody who'd use them.

When my first big-game hunting opportunity came across my path—or the sidewalk, actually—I jumped at it. I'd noticed my neighbor Pete was outside, so I wandered over to say hello. A few minutes into our conversation, he announced, "I'm taking my older son hunting for the first time."

"What are you hunting, and where are you going?" I replied, trying to stifle my immediate enthusiasm, which was usually reserved for special times with my wife or dining at all-you-can-eat places that serve prime rib and coconut cream pie.

Pete's face lit up as he described his special deer hunting spot.

Then I blurted out with all the subtlety of a giraffe in a shopping mall, "Hey, can I go with you?"

"Sure," he responded. "I have everything we'll need for hunting, but you'll need your own tent, food, rifle, and personal gear."

That sounded great to me. I had a little backpacking tent, a summer sleeping bag, and no idea that I'd need much else. "Okay, count me in!"

As I walked those 50 or so steps back to my house, several thoughts smashed into me head-on. *Okay, I just agreed to go deer hunting. I don't have a deer rifle. I don't know anything about big-game hunting. And I don't have much money. Wow, this trip will be great!*

I immediately called my father-in-law to tell him the exciting news. He's been a pistol, rifle, and shotgun enthusiast for many years, and he's a lifetime NRA member too.

"That's great!" he exclaimed. "What rifle do you plan to use?"

"I have no idea," I said. I didn't know a .243 from a .300 Winchester magnum. "Maybe I can borrow one."

Roy paused briefly and then said, "You know, I'll give you a Springfield A3O3 .30-06 rifle that I bought through the NRA years ago for 20 dollars. It'll do the job. Do you want it?"

"Great!" I exclaimed, not realizing what a gift it really was. I found out later it had a Mauser action—one of the best ever made and prized by people who "sporterize" rifles. It was a truly magnificent gift.

A week later, I picked up the rifle Roy had sent to a licensed firearms dealer (a legal requirement at the time) and brought it home.

Several weeks later, I passed the state-required hunter's safety class. Then I waited expectantly for another six weeks until deer hunting season opened. As I put my gear into Pete's four-wheel-drive at 3:30 in the morning, I kept trying to hide my exuberance by yawning. It didn't work. I said hi to Pete and his son, Michael, as I climbed into the vehicle. The four-hour drive was an all-about-Pete private session, and I had a front-row seat. Pete bragged about his hunting prowess and told us hunting stories. Michael remained pretty quiet. He and I didn't ask many questions. Since Pete apparently knew so much, I hadn't read up on hunting lore. I just expected that he'd help me if I shot a deer or needed help with something. I knew for sure that I could skin out a deer, having done taxidermy on a possum and pheasant on my parents' dining room table years earlier.

Pete parked at the end of a dirt road in a remote foothills area filled with pine and aspen trees.

"You go to the right," Pete said, immediately taking charge. "We'll go someplace else."

I loaded five rounds into my rifle and headed up the side of a hill, clueless what to do next. As the first rays of sunlight touched the treetops, I imagined that a herd of deer would greet me around each bend. In the distance, I heard a squirrel's chirp as I walked on a game trail that weaved around and up the sides of various hills and near small meadows. Before long I learned firsthand why hunters avoid wearing nylon jackets. Again and again branches brushed against me, and the fabric trumpeted my presence.

Fifteen minutes later, I found myself moving into timber that was more dense, and then the trail I'd followed branched off in several directions. *What do I do now?* I wondered, my frustration growing. *Which path should I take? Or should I just sit down here and hope a deer wanders by?*

Conflict arose within me. On one hand, I realized I didn't need to worry about proving anything to anybody. I could just enjoy all the beauty around me and view today like walking around in a park. On the other hand, I wanted to prove to myself—and to Pete—that I wasn't just a wannabe hunter. I desired to demonstrate that I really could be a hunter—like other guys I knew—and perhaps have my own hunting stories to tell someday.

I chose the right fork without any idea why, and I walked more slowly because my sweat was making me cold. I knew about the dangers of hypothermia from my Boy Scout days, but I'd never learned about the dangers of cotton clothing—how it retains moisture rather than wicking it away from skin. As a cold, west wind penetrated my clothing, I tried to remember what I'd heard a friend say about using wind correctly. *I want to be downwind of a prime hunting spot,* I thought.

Several hundred yards farther, as I rounded a bend, I sensed something was watching me. I stopped and tried to figure out why I felt that way or if I were just imagining things.

Then I saw him. A nice-sized buck stood at the edge of a meadow! He seemed as puzzled as I was. He stared at me from 150 yards away as though I were the first human being he'd ever seen. Maybe I was.

My adrenaline pumping and my hands shaking, I aimed at the heart area and squeezed the trigger.

Down he went!

I stood there dumbfounded, realizing this was a milestone moment in my life. I even forgot to work the bolt and put another round into the chamber in case the buck got up and started running. As I walked up to the deer, I felt elated...and sad. Elated because of what I'd just done; sad because until moments ago this majestic animal had been experiencing life in such gorgeous country.

Then a loud, piercing thought screamed for attention. *Now what am I supposed to do?*

I remembered from my hunter's safety class that I needed to gut the deer, so I straddled it and started cutting. It took me a while to figure out where to cut. Not having a small saw to cut up the center of the ribs and at his back end made my work harder. But my knife held up, and I completed the job in about 45 minutes. (I did everything right except I forgot to take out the windpipe.)

*Now what?* I looked at the deer as large snowflakes started to fall. *If only Pete were here.* Then a new thought emerged. *It's important to get the animal cooled down as quickly as possible.* So I skinned the deer right there in the forest. By the time I finished, my fingers felt colder than the snow all around me. Heat rose from the deer's cavity as additional snow fell.

I was tired.

After mentally retracing the path to the vehicle, I decided not to return the way I'd come.

"Uh-oh," you may be thinking, "this won't turn out well."

I thought, *I'll go down this hill and keep moving to the right until I come to the road. Then I'll walk to where Pete parked.* Since I didn't want to get my down jacket all bloody, I tied it around my waist, hoisted the deer around my neck, and headed downhill. Things went well (I thought) until I came to a small but steep ravine I couldn't cross. I stood there sweating as I tried to figure out my next move while balancing the deer on my shoulders. It seemed heavier and heavier—I'm sure it was because of all the snow collecting on it.

*I can keep walking downhill and hope this ravine ends or I can go back the way I came. Okay, I'll cut the deer in half and hang half of it in that pine tree within sight of that tall dead tree with the broken top. I'll carry the other half back up and walk to the Blazer the same way I came. Tomorrow I'll return to get the other half.*

(Stop laughing at me, okay?)

By the time I reached the road, I was quite a sight.

I was shivering.

My T-shirt was soaked with blood.

I wore a proud look on my face.

It felt mighty good to get the half a deer off my back and onto a tarp. Pete and Michael sat in the Blazer eating sandwiches.

"Why'd you skin the deer?" Pete asked, finishing his sandwich and drinking another sip of coffee. Criticism was obvious in his voice.

"I thought that's what I was supposed to do."

He grunted.

I was shocked by the anger and jealousy I heard in his voice when he commanded, "Get on the tailgate with the deer. I don't want you to get any blood on the seat."

As I settled in, he quickly took off, driving rather fast for about 15 minutes to where he planned to camp. The cold wind finished taking what little body heat I'd been able to retain. I kept wishing he'd stop so I could put on my jacket—blood or no blood. I was turning into a human Popsicle.

Twenty minutes later, I was starting a fire with damp wood, shivering almost too much to talk, while Pete and his son sat in the vehicle with the heater going full blast.

"So what are you doing?" he asked.

"Trying to get warm," I answered.

I don't remember much about that night, which is probably a good thing. But I did keep waking up and wondering how I'd find the other half of my deer someplace back in the woods.

To his credit, Pete drove me to the trailhead after breakfast the next morning, but he didn't say much. I got out and headed down the same trails, thankful I no longer had to carry my rifle. New, wind-blown snow had covered nearly all of my tracks, but I had enough memories to get me to the general area where I'd shot the deer.

Perhaps you know what happens when a novice hunter who grew up in the suburbs tries to find half a deer hanging six feet up from the ground in a thick pine tree in the middle of a large, dark forest. Some apt phrases come to mind.

Wandering in circles.

Looking for a specific tree with a broken top.

Getting cold…and colder.

Feeling angrier and angrier at myself.

Dealing with nearly frozen feet.

I finally discovered the dead-tree marker, yet I still couldn't find the carcass. "God," I prayed, desperation prominent and worry stewing inside me, "will you help me find my deer, *please*?"

Within 30 seconds, my eyes noticed a spot of blood on the snow. "Thank you, God!" I said aloud. It just didn't seem right to just think about thanking him.

By the time I returned to the vehicle, Pete was ready to go home. He and Michael had hunted for several hours and hadn't seen a good-sized buck with the required points. As I climbed in, it seemed that Pete was even more angry that I'd shot a buck and he hadn't. During the ride home, my host said little. In fact, he never brought up that hunting trip again. Not long after that, he pretty much avoided me.

When I got home, my wife, Amanda, more than made up for Pete's actions. She wanted to hear all about what happened. She smiled or gave me strange looks at the appropriate times during my story. Then she got out a cookbook that had pictures of where different cuts of meat were located on a cow, and we used that as a guide as we cut up venison in our little kitchen. We marked the freezer paper with "stew," "steaks," and "not exactly sure." (We didn't really use this last category, though we should have. In light of how chewy some of the meat was, it should have been marked "cook for 18 hours minimum.")

After several days had passed, I couldn't help but think about what had happened during my hunting trip:

- I was thankful I'd been able to shoot the buck.

- It felt great to have meat in our freezer.

- I'd learned valuable hunting lessons—about not wearing nylon, about avoiding cotton, about why it's not good to skin a deer before carrying it out, and why it's

not great to try shortcuts on the way back to the vehicle or camp. I also learned why I'd never again hunt with
someone like Pete, who cared more about his image as
a great hunter than he did about helping a beginner. (I
almost shiver in my office right now just thinking about
how close I came to becoming hypothermic after that
tailgate ride. Maybe I should put on a sweater.)

- Most important, God demonstrated his faithfulness to
me when I was about 10 minutes away from giving up
on finding the other half of that buck. The moment I
prayed that simple prayer asking for help, the God who
created the universe heard me and acted on my request.

Perhaps you're a bit like I was in those woods—searching for
something you can't find yet knowing it's there somewhere.

I've been there.

It can be hard to find what our hearts yearn for—perhaps some
kind of purpose and meaning that goes much deeper than possessions, fame, power, a rugged "I can do this on my own thank you
very much" statement, and so many other things our culture highly
values. That includes great hunting trips.

That day in the woods taught me a simple truth that has stuck
with me ever since and is especially comforting during painfully difficult times of searching and loss. I think you'll find it very benefi-
cial too.

Are you ready?

*Talk with God.*

See, I told you it was simple.

I picture God dancing with joy when we invite him to come
alongside us and help us carry the weight of fear, insecurity, anger,
lust, greed—and anything else that wounds us and holds us back
from experiencing his abiding presence and the life he offers us.

A friend of mine who works in advertising once needed to set up a photography shoot of a Christmas setting in the middle of a forest. He and a coworker packed in Christmas tree lights, a generator, gasoline, photography equipment, a ladder—everything they needed. Things went pretty well until they ran out of time at the end of the shoot. It got dark, and they had to leave all those lights on that tree. Quite likely they are still there today, waiting to confound a lone hunter.

I wish I could go back and find that tree where I'd hung that deer half. I'd put Christmas tree lights on it, fire up one of my generators to make it light up, and reflect on how God has answered some of my prayers since that deer hunt. It'd be like one of those Old Testament monuments—only a tree. You know, when the Israelites did what God told them to do: put up memorials of stones—standing stones—so they'd always remember the ways in which he demonstrated his character and helped them accomplish mighty things (Genesis 35:14; Exodus 24:4; Joshua 4:19-24). The Israelites were commanded to keep telling these stories to their children and grandchildren.

On second thought, it's much easier for me to pray right here, right now—to count my blessings from God (including the hard-fought ones that come as my heart finally softens) and remember God's promises—than to lug a generator into the woods.

# Ben's First Hunt

Rich, a friend of mine, told me this story. He and his son Ben said I could share it with you. I know you'll get a kick out of it.

———•———

One day I asked my then 12-year-old son, Ben, if he'd like to go hunting with me. I showed him photographs of some outings I've had, and his face came alive.

"Really?" he said. "You'd take me on a hunt?"

Brent, a friend of mine, belongs to a hunt club not far from where we live, and he has several 20-gauge shotguns for youth. One of them fit Ben perfectly.

So we picked a date to hunt birds. It was a pivotal time in my life. I'd been asking myself, *How am I passing the baton of things I enjoy to Ben, such as appreciating, respecting, and using firearms and the joy of hunting?*

Ben and I had already spent time together at shooting ranges using .22 rifles and shotguns. During those times, I showed him how to respect the weapons and handle them safely. I knew these times significantly impacted Ben. He felt important. Valued. Loved. And he realized I was passing on to him things that are important to me.

As the day approached for our hunting adventure, I bought him an orange vest and hat. We assembled all the gear we'd need.

On the day of the hunt, Ben was all eyes—quiet but excited. We put on layers of clothing and headed out to meet Brent at a little diner.

Brent has two trained bird dogs. They were kenneled in his truck and excited about going hunting too. After breakfast, we double-checked our gear to make sure we had everything—including extra shells. We rode with Brent to the hunt club, signed the required documentation and waivers, and got ready to head out.

First we did some trap shooting to "dial in" our shotguns. I hit several clay pigeons, and then it was Ben's turn. We discussed how to aim by moving with the clay pigeon and leading it a bit.

His first shot—a miss.

Brent and I encouraged him to try again.

His second shot—a miss.

Third time—smash! Pieces of clay went everywhere! He nailed the clay pigeon, and we were "high fiving" all around.

Fourth time—a miss.

On the next three shots, Ben nailed them all.

He was noticeably gaining confidence as he squeezed the trigger and put into practice everything he'd been learning for months.

Every time he'd hit a clay pigeon, Ben would look back at us, and we'd say, "*Yes!* Great shot!" He was doing fantastic.

When we were ready, we drove out to a harvested cornfield. Pheasants, chukars, and quail had been released here and were hiding among the stalks.

One at a time, we released a dog to go to work finding a bird. It was amazing to see the dogs' countenances change when they started to hunt. Their whole lives are about smelling and finding birds. I love watching their focus and passion. Suddenly all the muscles in their bodies tense up when they approach a bird. They're quivering yet being as still as they can.

After a dog found a bird, we'd approach and sometimes three or four birds would fly up. The first time this happened, Brent got several quail and I shot a chukar. The hunt was on!

Brent and I showed Ben how fast the shooting happens and what the birds look like when the dogs retrieve them.

We started down another area of the field. I was on one side of Ben; Brent was on the other.

The dog went on point. On command, he flushed a bird. Ben still wasn't sure what to look for and how to quickly dial in on the bird he wanted to shoot.

"It happened so fast!" Ben said.

"This is your quadrant," I explained as I showed him the parameters. "Anything within this area is yours to take."

"I got it," he said.

We had only walked 50 yards when the dog went on point again. This time the bird flushed—and again Ben didn't shoot. He'd forgotten to take the safety off.

"That's what this is all about," I told him. "I've gotten so excited that the same thing has happened to me."

Then a third bird flushed in Ben's area. He shot—and the bird fell!

"Dad, I got one!" he exclaimed. "I did it! That's my bird!"

"Look at how this happened," I said, walking him through the steps.

We looked at his chukar and took photographs of it.

Then things got even better. Ben shot a number of quail and another chukar. He missed several times, but got right back on focus and tried again.

Brent and I continued to go over basics with him—how to lead the birds a little bit, the importance of perseverance, and to not get discouraged.

The best moment of all occurred as we walked down one section. Desiring to focus on Ben, Brent and I left our guns behind. The dog got on point, and we watched Ben implement every piece of strategy he'd learned. He commanded the dog to flush and then shot the chukar that flew up. He was so excited about putting all the pieces together—the stalking, the watching, commanding the dog, shooting the bird, the dog retrieving the bird, taking the bird and putting it in the game pouch.

Ben was all smiles, and I had tears in my eyes because I got to see him experience this. That's what this day was all about. My son not only discovered what it's like to shoot birds, he also took another step in his journey toward becoming a man.

We took more photographs. Ben had succeeded! He had what it took to achieve what he wanted to accomplish. I was so thankful to be able to support him as he learned more about hunting. It was a joy to see him come alive as he experienced bird hunting.

We took the birds back to the clubhouse kitchen, and Ben participated in another part of the hunt—cleaning the birds, dealing with the blood, handling the smells.

Later, when we got home, Ben had the joy of bringing meat home and telling his mother all about the day's hunt.

Ben and I will never forget this hunt!

◆——◆

Ben's first bird hunting adventure says it all, doesn't it? A father teaching, guiding, and encouraging his son before, during, and after a precious hunting experience. And there was the added benefit of having a friend there to help out. Yes, it took time and cost money. And it started Ben off on what may be a lifetime of following a hunting path.

Some of us have sons or daughters who aren't interested in archery or shotgun and rifle shooting. That's okay. Every man can find opportunities to pass on, as Rich is doing, the important batons of knowledge, experience, and wisdom. Information about hunting and so many other aspects of life too.

We can demonstrate interest in whatever our sons and daughters are interested in. We can sacrifice time and money to spend time with them—talking about what they want to talk about, doing what they enjoy doing.

May each of us who are fathers take advantage of these opportunities. Our children grow up so quickly. And every one of them needs what we alone can provide—love, a listening ear, forgiveness, guidance, hope for the future, tips on relationships...

And if you're not a father, you can still help young people (and their fathers or mothers) learn about and experience the thrills of shooting and hunting. You can share wisdom and knowledge with your friends' kids or children in your church family.

I experienced this after Rich and Ben were shooting my .22 at my shooting range. Ben proudly showed me his target with a lot of holes "in the black." I'm sure I felt some of the emotions Rich was feeling as I encouraged Ben and told him I was proud of him.

Perhaps the next time Rich and Ben come over to shoot, I'll hear the sharp crack of a deer rifle...or perhaps the quiet thud of an arrow hitting a hay bale.

I can't wait.

# Four Huge Inches

Gary, a friend of mine, shared the following story, and he told me I could share it with you. I think you'll appreciate it!

———•———

My friend Jeff and I decided to archery hunt in September. We started practicing in July to become accurate up to a maximum of 60 yards, even though our usual shots at animals are between 20 and 40 yards. I practiced at home as well as at a range. To further hone our skills, Jeff and I did 3-D shoots at figures of deer and elk at various distances to better learn distance estimation and improve our accuracy.

We bought tags for either sex deer and also elk tags just in case we happened upon one.

On Friday, the day before our season opened, we left early and drove several hours until we reached a trailhead below timberline (about 9000 feet elevation) where we'd camped and hunted previously. No motor vehicles were allowed past that point.

We set up our tent and organized our gear so we could start early the next morning. Before sleeping, we rechecked and waxed the strings on our bows so they'd be quiet and repel water. We then headed to bed.

At five in the morning, we drank instant coffee and ate instant oatmeal before putting our lunches—jerky, apples, sandwiches—into our daypacks. After double-checking to ensure we had our hunting licenses, knives, and other essentials, we got our bows and arrows and headed out of camp.

Two trails several miles long—one going high, one going low—start at the trailhead. Jeff chose the high one; I took the lower one. We planned to remain in sight of one another whenever possible in case one of us caused animals to move toward the other person.

We started hunting immediately. Creeping along. Being really quiet. Watching anything and everything. I watched for hoofprints, droppings, bed areas…as I tried to figure out the animals' usual routes. Usually a bed area reveals how recently they've been there. I also listened for limbs breaking because it was pretty dry so I'd be able to tell if deer were moving in the area. I listened for squirrels. They'll chirp at everything, so if I'm careful and haven't scared them and they're chirping ahead of me, it's a sign something's up there.

Maybe an hour later, I saw three-day-old tracks but no bed areas. I stalked with anticipation, knowing fresh tracks might be less than 20 yards away although still unseen. Now, I don't just "nature walk" stalk—staying on the trail. I sneak off the trail 10 yards or so in one direction, and then move 10 yards in the other direction, covering as much ground as possible.

Around 9:30 I took a break—eating jerky, listening for deer, thinking about where the animals might be. Then I continued to stalk.

About noon, Jeff and I met where the trails converged above timberline, ate lunch, and took a relaxing nap in the sun for 45 minutes. We scanned the area with binoculars and discussed what we'd seen— no new sign. We started stalking down a lower trail in a ravine area. I was on the right side; he was on the left.

We threw out a few low cow calls occasionally; because it was really sunny, we didn't bugle. And we didn't get any replies. Maybe a quarter mile from camp, I glanced over…and could just barely see a doe off to my right, about 40 yards away, eating some kind of bush.

I only had a four-inch hole to shoot through!

She hadn't spotted me, so I decided to take the shot because of all the practicing I'd done. I let an arrow fly—and it went right through that hole! *This is great!* I thought. *I'm so glad I practiced so much.*

Jeff and I sat down to let the doe rest…and die. Fifteen minutes later, we walked to where I'd hit her. There was a big pool of blood, so I knew she wasn't far away. *All the work we've done has come together!* I pondered.

When I found the doe, I got to work with my knife. Jeff kept hunting as he swung by camp to pick up our meat-carrying packs.

Back at camp, we let the meat cool down overnight by hanging it up.

Early the next morning, knowing it'd warm up, we put ice in a cooler and added a layer of trash bags. We put the meat into cotton bags and placed them on the trash bags. That way no water touched the meat. We drained the cooler daily and kept it in the shade.

We kept hunting for the rest of the weekend, but we didn't shoot another animal. Optimistically we made plans to hunt the next weekend!

———

There's nothing like success when overcoming a challenge, is there? But all that practicing isn't easy. Doing something repetitively with commitment and a target objective in mind is often tedious and tiring.

In many instances, practice is a requirement for getting things right, not just when we're hunting but in daily life as well.

It takes practice to open up communication with a withdrawn teenager, a neighbor whose heart is hardened toward everyone, or a spouse who has been promised much and given little emotional support and love.

It takes practice to watch our words and continually encourage and affirm rather than accuse, create confusion, or put down.

It takes practice to evaluate our reactions and replace any anger, critical spirit, frustration, lust, or manipulation with authenticity, love, generosity, and transparency.

It takes practice to guard our thoughts and to constantly direct them toward positive thinking, to follow through with affirming actions, to receive joy from God, and to apply his wisdom from the Bible rather than habitually accusing, confusing, shaming, blaming, or dwelling on negatives.

These things are harder than shooting at a hay bale or 3-D animal figure. But staying uplifting and supportive in order to honor God and sincerely love people is an adventure and challenge we men need! And our loved ones will appreciate it too.

The rewards of our practice will be much greater than any good story or a freezer full of meat.

**4**

# Contentment

I just opened a hunting catalog from a well-known company. I've visited several of their showrooms and seen incredible mounted animals and special displays. I've admired their huge selection of firearms and ammo. Millions of dollars have been spent on my behalf and the thousands of other hunting enthusiasts who enter those doors. Each time I enter the aisles of this hunting Eden, I'm positive a little bird is sitting on my shoulder chirping, "Buy this! Try on that! You *want* it! You *need* it! You *deserve* it!" So many products entice me, including:

- Scent-reducing shirts that will miraculously trap my sweat and turn it into something else. (Really?)
- Shirts that dry in 15 seconds or less if I fall into a creek. (No, maybe 20 seconds. I'd better read the small print.)
- An infrared night-vision LED camera with motion sensors that I can mount along a deer path and record for up to six months the bucks I never see during hunting season.
- A handheld weather station that will tell me how high

I climb (up to 30,000 feet), barometric pressure, wind speed, wind chill, and other factors I can use to rationalize another 30 minutes of sleep on a frosty morning or one more cup of coffee before I leave my tent.

- A night-vision scope so instead of sleeping I can watch owls catching mice, and foxes eating rabbits, and elk moving to locations far from my hunting range.

- Battery earmuffs that can magnify a squirrel's shriek when I'm on stand or allow me to listen to my favorite radio stations instead of squirrels.

- Game bags that I can wash and reuse after they've been filled with bloody body parts. (But not in our washing machine, my wife tells me.)

- No-scent clothes soap that promises a trophy animal will come really close to me if I've washed my clothes with it (Even if I have chili the night before?).

How I've managed to live this long without these items is beyond me! And the catalogs keep arriving. Tantalizing specials. Discounts if I spend more money (even if it's money I'd planned to use for house paint, truck parts, and a new winch cable). I wonder how buyers might respond if the copywriters included this phrase on the covers of catalogs: "Emotion-Generating Items Designed to Reduce Your Contentment and Motivate You to Spend Money"?

Perhaps what's really going on is that I all too frequently return to the battleground between *needs* and *wants*. My patched down coat looks like I've worn it for 25 years. Probably because I have! The temptress calls out, "But what about that new 'extreme' coat with a visored hood, two-zippered security pockets, and shock-corded cuffs?"

My WWII-era, German wool pants with several holes in them have covered many miles but still work well on freeze-my-rear-off, minus 20-degree days. The temptress croons, "Not everyone appreciates this kind of unusual fashion statement."

The wool hat I wash too seldom has warmed my ears for years. The temptress sighs deeply and says, "Now you can get a polypropylene fleece one that represents the best in countering penetrating wind and cold weather."

Because I still use a leather rifle sling that probably dates back to the Korean War age, the temptress gently reminds me, "A nylon sling never needs saddle soap."

And there's my well-used backpacking tent that has withstood winds that blew the nylon ground-cover sheet right out from under me while I slept. The temptress croons, "You can't even stand up or turn around in it without having to go to the chiropractor. Check out this new tent with all the convenient features you've always wanted, including a third room that can be turned into a hot-tub room with the right location, digging tools, and utility hookups." (Okay, I added this last option.)

Sometimes reading or even skimming these hunting-related catalogs builds excitement and longing within me. Quite often, in fact. I catch myself thinking...

> *Wow! I no longer would need to take five rolls of duct tape, three rolls of tie wire, needles and thread, boot patches, and a mechanic who will keep my old truck running but eats too much during hunting trips.*

> *If I just replace my old gear with this new stuff, the hunters I meet on the trail or in camps will compliment me on the fact that my coat and pants are stylish and I use the latest technology. And then, by golly, I'll never see them again to compare smoke-scented outfits by the campfire.*

I'm not a betting man, but I'll still wager that the next hunting catalog I receive will also contain such descriptions as low-profile, automatic, guaranteed, perfect-for-extreme conditions, weather-resistant, durable, moisture-wicking, rugged... You get the picture (and probably the catalogs!).

And then come the offers presented via the photograph temptress. Photographs with just the right smiles on the campers' faces (even though it's the sixteenth take and mosquitoes are buzzing). There's no bacon grease along the edges of the propane stove and the table on which it sits. And don't forget the beautiful trophy deer hanging from the hitch hoist (no blood from the gut cavity allowed).

If we're not careful, the temptress captures our eyes…and our hearts and minds as well.

She promises that we'll always be successful hunters if we dial the 800 number and punch in the order code. She invites us to look just right, smell just right, shoot like snipers, stay warmer, and in other ways stand out next to a fake decoy on a pond as a hunter of distinction with class, significance, influence, and style.

She lies.

Fortunately I've been spared some stresses that hunting catalogs create because I was either too busy surviving financially to peruse some of them or the postal service delivered some of them to the wrong address. Come to think of it, I've even had better hunting adventures because of my time-tested (old) gear.

I've been able to pitch tents on snow and sleep in them for extended periods of time without a heater. (Aren't my leather boots and water jugs supposed to freeze solid every night?)

I've had unexpected opportunities to put on tire chains during blizzards when my vehicles couldn't make it up icy hills, and I've seen more terrain while grinding up mountain passes at such slow speeds that a cross-country skier could have passed me.

I've been in remote places I might not have seen if I hadn't needed to drag game out to the road to load into my pickup.

I've climbed countless ridges with boots that only let in a tiny bit of water with each step—and I still have my toes, though they sometimes turn blue when I see frigid winter scenes on television.

I've hiked down the wrong ridge and experienced the joy of testing my endurance while shivering as I backtracked to get to camp before dark. (Take that, expensive GPS units that are threatening to remove such lesson-teaching thrills from life.)

I've seen bright stars and hiked extra miles in the woods at night after my old, non-LED flashlight beam grew dimmer and dimmer on a trail before finally granting me the privilege of walking by beautiful moonlight.

Countless times my buddies and I have dragged animals through scrub oaks, ravines, up tall mountains, into low valleys, across dead logs…gaining far more muscle tone and lung capacity than we would have if we'd pulled out those animals with a winch-equipped ATV.

Given all these adventures and my ongoing desires for up-to-date gear, how can I focus on the right things and keep the right perspectives? What if someone offered to buy me a battery-powered ATV that quietly climbs mountains, easily negotiates icy trails, and has a winch that can hang the entire ATV plus two dead deer from a thick tree limb? I'd say, "No thank you." Well, I think I would.

Timothy wrote, "Godliness with contentment is great gain. For we brought nothing into the world, and we can take nothing out of it" (1 Timothy 6:6-7).

Jesus said, "Watch out! Be on your guard against all kinds of greed; life does not consist in an abundance of possessions" (Luke 12:15).

The author of the book of Hebrews wrote, "Be content with what you have, because God has said, 'Never will I leave you; never will I forsake you'" (Hebrews 13:5).

Perhaps you've experienced some of the same feelings I have. Here's one more verse that quietly provides the bottom line for so many issues if we trust in God. Paul wrote to the Philippian church: "My God will meet all your needs according to the riches of his glory in Christ Jesus" (Philippians 4:19).

I'm especially vulnerable to certain temptations. In fact, that's why I receive those catalogs. Grudgingly I admit that I'll probably be tempted to buy additional hunting gear until I breathe my last breath.

One morning I threw away an old canvas hunting tent I could see light through every time I put it up in decent weather. During rainy days, it would just leak.

My neighbor called me. "What's wrong with this tent on your garbage can?" he asked. "You never throw away anything good." When I started to list my 35 reasons for tossing it, he quickly interrupted, "Great! It's just what I need to cover our tomatoes to protect them from frost. Thank you!" And then he hung up.

Take that, Hunting Store Palace! You don't offer a 30-year-old, "only eighteen holes and a broken zipper" tent in any of your catalogs!

Come to think of it, maybe you and I should send those catalog gurus some of our time-tested gear that our hunting buddies and spouses have beseeched us to make disappear for years. But that might give the catalog temptress more adjectives to work with. And she might even invite us to pose with our gear for 35 niche catalogs showcasing well-used, time-tested gear even Goodwill wouldn't want.

After all, catalogs nowadays don't need more colors—they need more contrast.

# Unbelievably True

My friend Gary told me this great story, and he said I could share it with you. I'm sure you'll appreciate it.

———◆———

My buddy Jeff and his cousin left on Thursday to go archery hunting for deer and elk. I couldn't leave until late Friday. Each of us had two horses—one to ride, and one to carry gear.

Friday, after driving a few hours, I parked near Jeff's truck at the trailhead. I fed and watered my horses, fixed a quick dinner, and slept in my pickup. At dawn I loaded my gear on the pack horse, bridled and saddled my riding horse, locked up everything, and headed toward the hunting camp—about 10 miles away. I saw several deer but no keepers on the way, so I couldn't wait to really start hunting.

Suddenly I met Jeff and his cousin on the trail. They'd already killed two six-point bull elk and a five-point deer! Because it was so warm, they were hurrying to the trailhead to get the meat into coolers.

As I approached the camp close to dark, I was thankful to see the tent because I was really tired. I took care of my horses first, organized my gear, ate dinner, and went to bed. I set my low-noise alarm clock (you never know which animals might be around when you wake up at five o'clock).

When I woke up, I lit the little propane lantern, ate instant oatmeal, and had some coffee with a bit of hot chocolate added. I put on my camo, prepared lunch, got out my elk calls, and checked my 75-pound compound bow with a 50-pound release. I glanced over my three-vaned aluminum arrows with three-bladed razor broadheads.

I was super excited as I headed out looking for a four-point or better buck and at least a five-point bull elk. I began hunting behind the camp and did some tough climbing. The deer I saw were too high for me to approach and get a shot.

At noon I crawled under a tree, ate lunch, and took a nap (figuring most animals were napping too). There have been times when I've opened my eyes after a nap and found deer staring at me. I'm sure they were wondering what I was and what I was doing. But not this time. I saw fresh tracks and heard elk calling around me, but none were in sight.

I decided to call it a hunting day and go after them the next day when Jeff and his cousin returned to camp. Just before dark, we met up on the trail. We heard elk bugle in the woods nearby. The next morning they began bugling early. Jeff's cousin decided to go where I'd seen deer, while Jeff and I hurried to where we thought the elk were. I was eager to start calling a big bull right to us. When we got into position, we stalked forward slowly through the dark timber (dense forest with thick underbrush). I threw out cow calls; Jeff threw out bugles.

About 500 yards into the deep woods, the day became really exciting. Four bulls were answering us—and we could tell the oldest one by its deep groaning call. He believed Jeff was a bull trying to get his cows. In fact, we had moved within a large herd of elk. Cows were running all around us. A four-point bull ran right by not 15 feet away—and didn't seem to notice us.

Caught up in activities of the rut, those bulls were excited and crazy. As we started to hone in on the herd bull that was somewhere above us, a five-point bull passed us from below. He was going so fast I didn't even have a chance to raise my bow.

With cows milling around us, Jeff threw a "big bull call" out there. Immediately we saw movement above us. A six-point bull appeared, slowly walking toward us. We remained very still as he moved to our left and then crossed to our right. I figured he was about 40 yards away.

I went to full draw while Jeff kept calling. He was lying on the ground now, and I was on my knees…waiting…and waiting…for a good shot. That bull didn't cross in front of me. I was afraid to turn my head to look for him, so I glanced down at Jeff. He pointed behind me.

Out of the corner of my left eye, I noticed the bull only 20 feet away! He was coming toward us! He stopped about 10 feet in front of me, staring at me in bewilderment because he was ready to fight another bull.

Then the bull, now about two feet from Jeff and five feet from me, turned slightly. I released my arrow, hitting him hard in the side. He jumped, almost landed on Jeff, and then ran uphill about 100 yards before lying down.

I lay down, shaking a little. Jeff was shaking too. What a close encounter! After catching our breath, we glassed the elk. Both of us could see blood coming out of the bull's side. After lying down for about an hour, he stood up and moved off. Knowing we'd have a difficult time packing him out if he went into the next steep ravine, we followed him.

Jeff was in the lead as I got an arrow ready. We didn't want to spook him and have to track him for miles. Suddenly Jeff signaled me as he lay down. I followed suit and crawled up next to him. The bull was standing above us. I crawled to within 40 yards of him, raised up slowly from the brush, and shot again. My arrow hit the elk's heart, and he immediately fell over.

After carefully approaching him and making sure he was dead, we took photographs and then caped and skinned him. We loaded the meat onto the horses and headed back to camp, arriving just before dark. Because the temperature was too warm for the meat to be out very long, we headed to the trailhead the next day.

My friendship with Jeff became even more solid after that. We still talk about that adventure, and he remembers thinking, *Gary, shoot that bull now before it steps on me!*

What a great trip. The rack was big, but I never had it scored. It's my bull, and that's enough. I'm proud of it. It was phenomenal to be that close to such a huge animal and bring it down. Just telling this story gives me chills all over again.

———

Thinking about Gary's story and how that bull elk acted crazy and lost its cautious nature during mating season caused me to consider how human males sometimes act when we allow whatever we chase after passionately to distort our reasoning. We throw aside all logic, ignore when cautiousness would be prudent, and sometimes even cross the line when it comes to our values and commitments.

Many things can prompt such crazy and dangerous pursuits: fatigue, desire for power or fame, unresolved anger, loneliness, hunger for adventure, drive to recapture aspects of youth. The list of all the bait luring us to dangerous ground and encouraging us to forget what's really important is long.

The pursuit of money can be at the expense of relationships. The illicit pursuit of a woman, allowing fantasies of women, or being involved with pornography creates unbridled passion, unrealistic desires, and sexual sin. The accumulation of possessions—and the identity we're trying to portray through them—promote deceit, pride, and unhealthy competition. Such pursuits make us incredibly vulnerable, just like that bull stopping five feet from Gary's nocked broadhead. Passion can blind us to who we have been and who we're striving to become. Temptations promise satisfaction but they lead to painful consequences and sometimes even death.

In a sense, the devil—the "evil one"—considers every day to be open season on our hearts and minds. He will use any weapon available against any or all of our weaknesses to cause us to turn away from God and his truth. The apostle Paul was deeply aware of this struggle:

> I know that good itself does not dwell in me, that is, in my sinful nature. For I have the desire to do what is good, but I cannot carry it out. For I do not do the good I want to do, but the evil I do not want to do—this I keep on doing. Now if I do what I do not want to do, it is no longer I who do it, but it is sin living in me that does it (Romans 7:18-20).

What consequences can wrong pursuits create? Envy. Discord. Impurity. Shame. Lack of self-control. Immorality. Self-hatred. Destroyed relationships. Wounded spirits. And many more.

Bucks and bulls react by instinct during the rut, but we humans have the ability and responsibility to make right choices.

- We can choose to acknowledge our weaknesses, wrong desires, and temptation to cast caution to the wind and do crazy things.

- We can choose to put up deterrents and defenses *before* dangerous-but-enticing pursuits dangle in front of us or creep up behind us.

- We can choose not to allow sinful desires to grow within us (James 1:13-14).

- We can seek God's wisdom found in his Word and use it to guide our steps.

- We can guard our hearts (Proverbs 4:23).

- We can believe that the rewards of our sacrificial choices to honor Jesus and our faith in him are worth every bit of our efforts.

- We can keep our eyes focused on Jesus, consciously and passionately working to do the right things he desires us to do knowing he will empower us to follow through (1 John 3:7).

Unlike such animals as deer and elk, we don't face a few weeks of instinctual craziness every year. No, our challenge is to be on guard against temptation 24/7. Perhaps that's why Paul wrote: "Be on your guard; stand firm in the faith; be courageous; be strong. Do everything in love" (1 Corinthians 16:13-14).

6

# Life on Self-Center

One minute I'm skinning an animal; the next minute my thumb is sliced open. Staring at the injury, I called my longtime hunting buddy Walt to my side.

"Why'd you do that?" he asked.

I didn't answer his right-to-the-point question because I wasn't pleased about my answer.

My brand-new Buck knife did a great job in the wrong hands.

"Wrong hands?" you ask.

I've skinned many small- and big-game animals, so I've become pretty fast at the task. Before we break camp, I usually skin and bag most or all of the animals for the entire group. That plus pride created my current problem.

I secretly fancied myself to be the camp's MDAS—"Modern-Day Animal Skinner." I'd desired to demonstrate my skinning prowess to my two hunting buddies, who really didn't care about speedy skinning. After using peroxide and placing butterfly bandages on the deep gash, I put on plastic gloves and finished skinning.

But I paid a steep penalty for my pride that day—much more than just a scar. I'd cut nerves. A week later, I suddenly lost feeling in much of that thumb. I frantically called the offices of about 10 neurosurgeons until I found a "gatekeeper" receptionist who recognized my sincere desperation. My high-pitched cries for help, deliberately toned down a little bit, no doubt communicated volumes. I made an appointment for later that day. When I arrived, I was led to an examination room. When the doctor arrived and looked my injured thumb over, he declared in a professionally practiced and comforting tone, "We can fix this right up for you." Then he hesitated, glanced at the paperwork, and asked, "How old are you?"

When I answered, he nearly laughed aloud and fell off his stool. "In that case, live with it. Usually some nerves connect naturally after a knife cut like this. Thankfully it's on the side of your thumb that isn't used often."

*A double hit below the belt,* I thought. *First, pride fueled my actions that resulted in unnecessary injury. And now I'm too old to have my thumb repaired properly?* I felt like I was being told to "move this heap into the barn where it will be out of the sun and rain. Put some mice poison around the seat cushions, lock it up, and leave it forever."

What did I learn from this experience? First, when entertaining visions of grandeur, don't have a Buck knife in your hand. Second, frequently check to make sure pride hasn't stalked or raced into your life or heart. Has pride wormed its way into your heart and mind the way a no-see-um gets through tent-door screens in Maine or water finds its way into a "waterproof" boot 15 minutes into your goose or duck hunt? Have you considered the ways you describe times when you've killed a game bird or animal from quite a distance? Or how far you crawled to get a great shot? Or how it only took one shot to bring a beast down? Or how skilled you are at picking game trails? Yep, I've discovered that my pride has leaped into all of those scenarios.

So much in our culture reinforces and values pride. How would people react if…

- a well-known hunter/lecturer declares in his full-color brochure and on his website, "Really, I'm just an average hunter who misses quite a few shots, but we edit those out of our videos and promotional materials."

- the manager of a hunting lodge states, "One third of the hunters who stay here shoot their animals; the rest don't. But our bunk beds are comfortable, and we provide cheese for the mousetraps in our sleeping rooms."

- an outfitter proclaims, "Take your chances! For $1000 a day, we guarantee a view of a canvas tent and a home-made outhouse you'll never forget, especially if the weather is lousy. Yes, it does rain more than 300 days a year here, so bring lots of waterproof gear."

- a hunting rifle manufacturer proclaims, "This one-of-a-kind rifle is at least as good as our competitors' rifles, and it only costs $100 more."

I've noticed that I'm not the only guy to reap the consequences of pride. The Old Testament recounts many stories in which pride led to negative consequences.

Powerful King Uzziah became so pride-filled that he deliberately disobeyed God by entering the temple to burn incense, which was a task assigned only to men descended from Aaron, of the tribe of Levi. The consequence he faced? Uzziah contracted a skin disease, so he was confined in a house and relieved of all responsibilities until his death (2 Chronicles 26:16-21).

Haman, the right-hand official of the Persian King Xerxes, offered to give Xerxes the equivalent of 375 tons of silver in exchange for permission to kill all the Jews in the kingdom (Esther 3:8-10). Haman boasted of his treasures and high position to his wife and friends (5:10-11). Haman's ultimate demise? He was impaled on a pole (7:9-10; some Bible translations read "hanged").

King Nebuchadnezzar praised himself: "Is not this the great Babylon I have built as the royal residence, by my mighty power and for the glory of my majesty?" (Daniel 4:30). The consequences? He went mad and lost his kingdom for seven years (4:31-36).

King Saul—who was very handsome and stood a head taller than everybody in his country—arrogantly disobeyed God (1 Samuel 13:7-15; 15:12-28). He also became angrily jealous of David when the Israelites praised the young shepherd more than him (18:6-9). What happened to Saul? God's Spirit left him. Saul took increasingly desperate measures to maintain his standing. Eventually he was badly wounded in battle and died.

Getting back to my thumb injury, what were some of the consequences I faced? The money I paid the neurosurgeon might have bought a rifle scope guaranteed to help me place five bullets into a dime-size hole at 400 yards when everyone on the shooting range is watching. Or I could have bought a five-year supply of the newest, hottest, copper-plated, boat-tail bullets that would be better than other hunters have.

*Oops!* Pride surfaces again!

If I shoot a huge buck possessing more Boone and Crockett points than a barrel cactus, I hope I use the words "pretty good animal" when describing him later. I also hope I'll show you a two-inch by two-inch photo of that buck—and *only* if you ask about it. And leave it at that.

I may not, unfortunately.

I trust that you'll understand.

Let's battle pride issues together. The scar on my thumb still speaks eloquently and forcefully about the dangers of pride—and may give me a head start.

# Dad and Daughter

As the dad of a delightful five-year-old daughter named Caitlin, I found myself trying to figure out how to encourage her to enjoy the outdoor activities her mother and I enjoyed. The most natural way Amanda and I did it was by doing things as a family.

We hiked in the woods.

We ice skated on ponds.

We slid down hills on sleds.

We camped next to a creek where our daughter guided pieces of wood through all the twists and turns of the "rapids."

One afternoon I took Caitlin fishing. I'd hoped to give her pointers about worms, hooks, bobbers, and casting. Instead I learned about questions. Picture us unloading the car near a small reservoir.

"Daddy, do I have to keep wearing my coat?"

"Yes."

"Is this where we're going to fish?"

"Yes."

"Will the wind keep making those white marks on the waves?"

"I hope not."

"Where are the fish?"

"I don't know."

"What are those red things, and what do they do?"

"Salmon eggs. The fish might want to eat them instead of the worms. When they do, we'll catch them!"

"Really?"

"I hope so."

"You didn't cast very well, did you, Daddy?"

"No!"

"What's this under this rock?"

"A crayfish."

"What's it doing?"

"Hiding, I guess."

"Why?"

"I don't know."

"Will I catch a fish on my line like you did?"

"I hope so."

"Want to hold a ladybug?"

"Not now. Thanks anyway."

"Can I go to the bathroom?"

"*What?*"

"Daddy, when you caught your fish, why did you say, 'We caught *him*'? Why not 'We caught *her*'?"

Nonstop questions came while I tried to accomplish important tasks, such as watching for strikes, untangling line, and putting sunscreen on our noses and necks. Obviously Caitlin was having a wonderful time.

Later, having experienced lots of fun fishing, I decided to introduce her to hunting—a little at a time.

She touched the wet hide of a freshly killed deer and looked at its eyes.

She touched the feathers of a goose.

She looked at an elk hanging from a meat pole.

She expressed interest in having a BB gun, so I bought her one and taught her to hit cans.

She desired to shoot my .22 rifle, so we went down to our home-made gun range on our property. I taught her the rules of firearm safety and praised her improving marksmanship.

Again and again, she passed little milestones I believed were motivating her to become my *Great Daughter the Hunter*.

I looked forward to the time when we'd get out in the field and bag a deer together, bonding as we put the liver in a plastic bag and wrapped the carcass in a breathable game bag to keep away flies.

Experiencing nature's dirt, mud, snow, sleet, and sun.

Spending hours pitting ourselves against wily creatures.

Shivering together on a deer stand before sunrise.

You get the point.

Finally I thought she was ready. A pronghorn hunt seemed like a perfect way to start. I'd held off asking her for years because I didn't want it to be a pressure thing, but I decided the time was right. So I asked her, and she said *yes*. But she didn't want to actually shoot a gun. She just wanted to go with me.

I *thought* that was fine with me.

We headed east on a Friday afternoon, our tent and gear in the truck. By five o'clock we'd arrived at our hunting spot, set up the tent, gotten things organized, and were figuring out the schedule for the next day.

When I mentioned a 5:30 wake-up time, she gave me *the teenager look* that communicated, "No way am I doing that as tired as I am."

Being the amazing dad that I am, I tried to cajole, change her mind, share the benefits of getting up so early (there weren't many), and even shame her a little so she'd get up early...all to no avail.

"Okay," I finally said, *really* listening to her. "I'll come back and get you after I've tried the first strategy. Sure you won't reconsider?"

"I'm sure."

When my alarm went off, I tried to be as quiet as possible (being the amazing dad that I am) as she snuggled deeper into her sleeping bag.

I felt a real sense of disappointment. *Wow, have I raised a daughter who won't hunt...not even with me?*

When I returned to camp two hours later, having not taken a shot, she was awake...and enjoying the companionship of a herd of cows.

"Are you ready to head out with me soon?" I asked, my hope jar brimming.

"No," she answered. "I'm really tired. I think I'll just stay here and read and sleep."

I don't recall what I muttered as I headed out again...or maybe I still want you to think I'm an amazing, wonderfully accepting dad who can handle every curve and dashed hope thrown at me. I ended up shooting my pronghorn—and Caitlin wasn't there to see it happen. And when I got back to camp, she remained pretty well crashed out.

My dreams of hunting geese, wild pigs, elk, deer, prairie dogs, coyotes, ducks, pheasants, and maybe an "exotic" or two with her were vanishing. *I didn't have anybody to teach me how to hunt when I was her age,* I thought. *She should be glad I want to show her. Why isn't she jumping at the chance to hunt with me?*

Caitlin and I had good conversations on the way home—mostly about non-hunting things: school, boys, teachers, athletics.

After that outing, she decided not to hunt.

I kept my devastated feelings to myself mostly, but I sometimes tried using camouflaged conversations. As we'd be doing something together, for some reason every once in a while the topic of hunting would come up and I'd drop a subtle hint. You know, like, "Hey, Caitlin! How about going hunting with me next weekend?"

No dice. Didn't work. Same answer every time.

"No thanks, Dad."

So I let go of my dreams, aspirations, manipulations...and gave up the idea of hunting with her.

And you know what happened? She and I started to communicate much better. She must have sensed I'd dropped my agenda and was ready to appreciate honest conversations with her much more. She needed her dad to listen to her, not just try to get her to do something he wanted to do.

As time passed, wonderful things began to happen. She started camping with friends, having grown to appreciate such activities with her mother and me. She appreciated the camping gifts I gave, even a tent I found at a thrift store.

While enjoying a weekend with experienced friends who hunted on a private wildlife ranch, she borrowed one of their shotguns—the first time she'd handled one—and amazed them with her excellent shooting. The looks on their faces, she recalls, were priceless.

For fun, she went pistol shooting with a young married couple.

Now grown and self-supporting, she prefers target shooting with a pistol above almost everything else except snowboarding and being with her boyfriend. And yesterday she brought him out to our property to shoot too.

Based on this progress, I fully expect she will begin hunting with me within the next six years, six months, and eight days.

Yeah, right.

Seriously…maybe she will.

Even if she doesn't, I'm thankful she understands my passion for the adventures of hunting. I'm glad she continues to enjoy many outdoor activities, some of which she does with me.

About a week ago, Caitlin reminded me of something I wish had never happened. "Dad, remember how you quit fishing with me because I lost too many of your expensive lures?"

Gulp.

I believe it's important for each of us to ask, "What's keeping me from inviting my child or grandchild to spend time with me and from doing what he or she wants to do?" Paul wrote to the church in Corinth, "Love is patient, love is kind. It does not envy, it does not boast, it is not proud. It does not dishonor others, it is not self-seeking, it is not easily angered, it keeps no record of wrongs. Love does not delight in evil but rejoices with the truth. It always protects, always trusts, always hopes, always perseveres" (1 Corinthians 13:4-7).

You see, life and love is not all about us. It's about sacrificially giving of ourselves to be available to our children, to our other family members, and to our friends…allowing them to be who God created them to be. To love them and really accept them for who they are. How can we do that? By encouraging them in their interests, whether or not it includes shooting big game or a game bird. Let's remember these three things:

- When our children desire our company, that's a blessing.

- When our children desire to do activities *we'd* prefer to do, that's a bonus.

- If the future with our children doesn't include hunting adventures, another type of quest will come along with our names on it.

Years ago I attended a parenting seminar. I don't remember much of what the speaker said, but I recall one important concept: *club time*. He encouraged dads to set aside time to do something special with their sons and daughters. And for husbands to set aside time to be with their wives—and only their wives (no kids!). I went home and implemented this idea.

Today my daughter still remembers our Club Times—and so do I. They comprise some of our best memories of being together. The funny thing is that we often didn't *do* a whole lot. We just hung out together. I tried to make every moment special for her and to let her know I loved her. Can you guess what happened? The adage "What goes around comes around" came true. I had way more fun being with her than I had when I scripted our activities to reflect my interests.

Do you have one-on-one "Club Times" with your children? The memories you're creating together will last for a long time. If you don't, perhaps it's time to experiment with the idea a few times. When you do, be ready for growing opportunities to encourage and enjoy your child's uniqueness. Try this even if your current relationship is strained or difficult. You may be surprised at what a relaxing, "no expectations" focus on your child and doing what he or she enjoys can accomplish.

Maybe after Caitlin reads this chapter, she'll say, "Gee, Dad, even before I read it, I was thinking about how I'd like to experience the joys of hunting—what I'd learn, how bloody my fingernails might get if I shoot one, the opportunities I'd have to wear all my jackets at the same time because of the intense cold…maybe even have the chance to help you put tire chains on your old truck or eat a granola bar for lunch washed down with cold coffee. What do you say?"

# Worn-Out Boots and Another Tale

Moments ago I looked in the entry closet and picked up my olive-green Sorel hunting boots with wool liners. My wife has been coaching (meaning "urging passionately") me to get rid of gear I no longer need, so for about five seconds I considered throwing away my Sorels.

They certainly don't look like much.

The left boot has a bicycle tire patch shadow over a penny-sized crack that opened up at a crease, but the patch wouldn't stay on. Both soles are worn down. The leather is faded and caked with sealant.

If boots could talk, these Sorels would describe many adventures and hunting stories that might keep an entire Boy Scout Troop laughing or curled up in fright inside warm sleeping bags.

I wore these boots when I went deer hunting with my friend Walt. We drove my '62 Willys Jeep. It had a steel I-beam for a bumper, an old 8000-pound Warn winch, a red-and-white paint job I proudly did myself with foam brushes, and a heater from a huge military truck. The Willys was so unusual that I sometimes wonder if I should have driven it to Los Angeles to sell to somebody who owned a beach-front condominium. The Jeep would be perfect as a one-of-a-kind trophy vehicle to cruise the streets and park anywhere without worrying about "bumper taps." (Take that, Mercedes, BMW, and Ferrari!)

On this particular trip, Walt and I eagerly left around four in the morning and drove three hours or so to a small mountain community on the edge of a national forest. We stopped in to visit a friend's father who handled maintenance for the homeowners' association there and knew the area well. After talking a bit and gaining insights on where to hunt, we took off down a dirt road.

When we got to the suggested hunting area, we discussed our deer-hunting strategies and then split up. I was wearing my usual military-surplus wool pants, long johns, several layers of shirts and coats, a wool cap underneath the legally required orange hat, and my green Sorel boots. It was snowing lightly, and the temperature was just below freezing.

As I stalked for deer on a game trail in the stillness of the woods, I thought about the relationship Walt and I had developed during our hunting adventures. I almost chuckled aloud while thinking that I, who grew up in a non-hunting family in a little suburb of Chicago, was now standing in six inches of snow hoping a big buck would pass by.

Not seeing fresh tracks or even a glimpse of a deer, I picked a spot with good visibility on three sides and sat down on my little waterproof sitting pad that usually reduces the impact of melting water on my anatomy. *Finally*, I thought, *I'm hunting again after months of wishing this day would arrive!*

The strong northwestern wind blowing through the dense aspen trees loosened snow that had piled up on branches, and down it came with a plop—right on my head. I brushed off the wet stuff, zipped up my jacket, and settled in for a long wait. Conditions were still ideal for stalking, yet I was enjoying this spot where ravines converged in the dark timber. Even in such an ideal setting, I found myself second-guessing my choice of spots. *What if I go a little farther north or nestle into a hidey hole at the top of the ravine to my right? What if the wind shifts direction again and carries my scent toward the area I'm watching? What if a cooperative buck doesn't choose to walk past me and offer to become breakfast sausage, hamburgers, and steaks?* I decided to apply a good friend's fishing advice to my hunting strategy. When I asked him how he caught so many fish, he replied, "I keep my line in the water." So I was keeping my rifle ready while waiting expectantly. I was listening, shivering, and daydreaming in that beautiful hollow. Just as my rear end started to go numb, I saw movement out of the corner of my eye. Three does…two more does…four more does were angling down a draw toward me. My heart pounding, I shifted position slowly and prepared to shoot. *Is there a buck around?* I wondered. I waited a bit longer.

Finally a wary buck showed his head about 40 feet behind his does. Evidently he'd picked up an amazing life principle: If something bad were to happen, he didn't want it to happen to him. *What an intelligent coward!* I observed as I sighted in on him.

Looking more like a low-profile snowman (and feeling nearly as cold) than a hunter, I waited until he was within 40 snowy yards and fired one shot. Off all the deer ran…including the buck. He hadn't even missed a step!

Dejected because my deer hadn't dropped, I stood up, shook off the snow, and gathered my gear. *I can't believe this. How'd I miss? Is there a blood trail?* At that point I hadn't done enough hunting to realize that even mortally wounded animals can travel quite a ways.

I needn't have worried.

Seventy yards away, just over a small rise, a blood trail six inches wide mottled the snow. Eighty feet farther, I found the buck just on the other side of a downed tree. I field dressed him and dragged him toward the Willys. All the way I was thankful for the traction and warmth provided by my Sorel hunting boots (you knew I'd mention them again).

Something unexpected happened as I approached the vehicle. A young boy walked up to me. His parents had evidently sent him out to me with a "message to the tall guy dragging a deer": "Hey, why don't you just buy hamburger at the grocery store?"

I was quite tempted to respond, "Well, considering the cost per pound of my deer after I add up money for two tanks of gas, the hunting license, the gun, the ammo, and other supplies, where can I get hamburger for less than eight dollars a pound?"

Figuring the young boy wasn't prepared to pull out a calculator or talk about venison prices, I wisely said nothing as I finished dragging the deer to the rear of the Willys.

Because my Sorels speak loudly of such stories, year after year they survive the "closet purge." In fact, they remind me of an important lesson too. As our Creator, God wants you and me to know him and remember what he has done throughout history and what life is like when we walk in close relationship with him. The word "remember" shows up again and again in the Bible. And I know that God certainly knows me inside and out. He is well aware of times I've questioned whether or not he knows and cares about what's happening to me or to those I love. He understands that I'm not always sure to what extent he still handles the important details of life on earth. Right now, in fact, my wife and I are walking closely with him after the devastating Black Forest Fire burned most of our property ( June 2013). Thankfully our house was spared. As if the consequences of the fire weren't enough to handle, we now face serious flash flooding every time it rains because the brush, trees, and other plants were torched. During this time of going from crisis to crisis—from shoring up our road to helping our neighbors who lost their homes—God guided me to a special passage in his Word. Isaiah 40:27-31 emphasizes that God knows everything and gives strength to the tired and power to the weak:

> Why do you complain, Jacob?
>> Why do you say, Israel,
> "My way is hidden from the LORD;
>> my cause is disregarded by my God"?
> Do you not know?
>> Have you not heard?
> The LORD is the everlasting God,
>> the Creator of the ends of the earth.
> He will not grow tired or weary,
>> and his understanding no one can fathom.
> He gives strength to the weary
>> and increases the power of the weak.
> Even youths grow tired and weary,
>> and young men stumble and fall;
> but those who hope in the LORD
>> will renew their strength.
> They will soar on wings like eagles;
>> they will run and not grow weary,
>> they will walk and not be faint.

I'm so glad that Amanda and I, along with all other followers of Jesus, aren't alone when facing serious challenges. Years before I bought my Sorel boots, I often sang the chorus from an old hymn called "Count Your Blessings," written by Johnson Oatman Jr. back in 1897:

Count your blessings, name them one by one,
Count your blessings, see what God hath done!
Count your blessings, name them one by one,
And it will surprise you what the Lord hath done.

Just like my Sorels remind me of so many hunting adventures, thinking about the blessings I've received from the Lord jolts my heart and mind into thankfully remembering what God mercifully and lovingly has done for me so far. It's quite a list, so here are just a few.

- Bringing me through two terrible car wrecks in which people driving their cars at extremely high rates of speed rear-ended and totaled my vehicles while I was stopped.

- Enabling me to walk again after serious back surgery (though a friend honestly stated that I walked like Frankenstein for a while).

- Giving me a wonderful family and friends who encourage me in remaining on God's path and the adventures that unfold around each bend.

- Providing memorable hunting trips.

- Comforting me when my mother and cousin died, reminding me that my time here is temporary and that heaven will be amazing.

- Protecting me during hours of riding with law enforcement officers as their chaplain.

- Empowering me to kick an alcohol habit more than 30 years ago.

- Increasing my opportunities to trust him and deepen my faith.

- Protecting me from marriage-destroying traps.

- Loving me no matter what.

- Enabling me to escape the previously mentioned forest fire that reached our property before firefighters were on the scene. The temperature exceeded 2400 degrees F.

Everywhere I've worn these old Sorel boots God has walked with me. No doubt about it—I'm keeping these boots...at least for another year.

I wonder if Amanda would understand my line of reasoning if I likened these boots to the standing stones the ancient Israelites erected to commemorate God's faithful presence and mighty acts (Deuteronomy 27:1-8; Joshua 4:1-9)? Or maybe the tassels he commanded the ancient Israelites to wear on their clothing in order to remember to obey all of his commands (Numbers 15:37-41)? Maybe I could even mount these Sorels permanently on a lazy Susan gizmo that spins around and around. We could use them as a centerpiece on the dining room table during special occasions. That would surely spark some hunting conversations!

Hmm...on second thought, I'd better keep the Sorels hidden in the closet.

# 9

# Surprises

One of the many things I appreciate about hunting is the way deer, elk, pronghorn, pheasants, ducks, geese…seem to suddenly appear out of nowhere or at least when we don't expect to see them. Whether we are novices or well-seasoned hunters with wrinkles from the sun, such moments are definitely exciting.

A friend of mine, Steve, grinned as he described a special goose-hunting trip. He and a few other hunters had hired a guide to get them to a great spot. After putting out more than 100 decoys, the guide directed them into blinds over which wooden covers had been placed. The idea was that when geese flew in, the hunters would move the covers and start shooting.

Things went even better than they'd hoped. Not only did flocks of geese fly in, they literally landed on top of the boards and started walking around! Needless to say, Steve and the other hunters experienced great shooting opportunities *after* they got the geese to move off the covers.

I experienced an amazing surprise a few weeks ago with a younger friend. During the past few months, Mike had developed a strong interest in hunting. You should have seen the joy on his face when I helped him find a rock-solid Winchester bolt-action .270 rifle at a gun show. Hardly able to contain his excitement, he soon came over to the house to dial in his bore-sighted 3 x 9 power scope at the 100-yard range I have set up on our property.

Upon learning that I was heading east of town to hunt a pronghorn during the first rifle season, he exclaimed, "Hey, I'd like to go with you on Saturday!"

"Sounds great!" I answered, knowing he'd never been big-game hunting. He and his father were going hunting for pronghorn in Wyoming in a few weeks, and neither of them had ever shot a large animal and experienced the joy—and work—of what happens afterward.

I remembered how hard it was when I first started to hunt. Nobody in my family—or extended family—hunted, so I had to learn from neighbors, friends, authors of hunting books, and trial and error the attitudes, skills, and knowledge that contribute to the love of hunting and appreciation of God's creation. (It's been great though, and I've garnered some lifelong memories from adventuresome hunting.) I welcomed the opportunity to spend special time with Mike to teach him some of the skills I'd learned.

A few days before opening day, I laid out the clothing I needed, including a heavy fleece jacket. I knew all too well how a cold wind can sweep across the ranch lands, biting my ears and fingers and trying to find places to invade. Or, in contrast, the temperature could be nearly 70 degrees with no wind. I've experienced so many weather changes even during one winter hunting day that I almost expect any kind of weather—sunshine, rain, snow, and sleet. I added a rifle cleaning kit, one-piece cleaning rod, and camera lens-cleaning tissues for my scope to the pile. Dust and dirt are enemies of fine optics.

On opening day when my alarm clock boldly announced it was time to get up, I eagerly hopped out of bed, grabbed a bite of honey-coated, carb-filled cereal, downed two cups of coffee, and then drove my old Honda with 370,000 miles on it to Mike's house across town. Since we weren't going off road and I had only one tag, I figured I'd save money on gas by taking the car rather than my pickup. I tied a two-wheeled box carrier to the roof rack to help us move the pronghorn I hoped to shoot.

As we drove the hour and a half to our hunting area, Mike asked me many questions about hunting, including what gear to carry in his daypack. I think I enjoyed that time as much as I enjoyed actually hunting during the rest of the day.

Each of us, as we learn to hunt more effectively, may have opportunities to share our enthusiasm for hunting with others—spouses, friends, neighbors, coworkers, grandchildren, children. One-to-one relationships are powerful and dynamic, impactful, and strategic learning opportunities especially now when self-focus and "it's all about me" attitudes prevail.

Years earlier, I would have arrived at a new hunting area long before first light—or been mad at myself for slacking off. This day, though, I planned to arrive mid-morning.

Why?

True to the weather forecast, a rare light rain during this period of drought had frozen overnight. Fog enveloped the entire area. Also,

I didn't know where the pronghorn were. I'd seen a buck with three does standing in a field six weeks earlier during my scouting trip. No doubt that field had been harvested, and probably everything was now dirt—literally.

I also didn't feel like sitting on the edge of a field by a fence post getting colder and hoping a pronghorn would be within range as the sun came up. I've done that—and gotten pronghorn—but it happened on a ranch we knew well, we were camped there, and we'd observed pronghorn movement the previous evening.

It hadn't been easy to gain the privilege of hunting this area today. Weeks earlier, I'd spent hours going from ranch to ranch, seeking owners who would allow me to hunt pronghorn on their land. Most of the ranches had gone "outfitter," meaning they received payments from outfitters for exclusive hunting rights. Many outfitters charge clients a small fortune to hunt in these "private" hunting areas.

Finally I met and spoke with the two adjoining landowners who agreed to let me hunt—after nearly an hour and a half of chatting over coffee, during which I emphasized my commitment to obey any rules they might set. I wondered if they were going to ask me to sign over the title to my hunting truck to close the deal. Too many previous hunters had broken ranch rules—leaving gates open, driving over crops, tossing trash onto the ground—so the ranchers were leery, almost a bit angry. Plus, a prolonged drought had damaged crops and dramatically increased the fire danger.

Our hunting area this day encompassed about 3500 acres of mostly flat land with maybe ten trees. If you have hunted only in densely timbered forests that receive lots of precipitation, this may sound like lots of land. But a few square miles of virtually treeless property isn't much for pronghorn.

As soon as we arrived at the hunting area, Mike and I checked in with both ranchers to let them know we were there and hear any final instructions. One rancher told us, "If you have any questions about boundaries, just call me. I'll be glad to drive over and show them to you." The other rancher invited us in for coffee, so we talked with him and his wife for 20 minutes and reviewed the map of hunting boundaries he'd given me during my scouting trip.

Fortunately the fog lifted during our chat. Mike and I slowly drove down ranch roads around each section (640 acres each), using our binoculars often. To my surprise, no pronghorn appeared. The more we drove, the more surprised I was. Usually pronghorn ran in herds this time of year, and not seeing even one animal startled me.

Although I didn't admit it, my hope of seeing a pronghorn faded as we scrutinized many hidden corners and ravines. Since we were hunting a doe for meat and not a trophy buck, I'd thought we'd have an easier time. I couldn't understand where the does were. Usually multiple does accompany a buck.

I thought about the time and money I'd invested in this trip. I didn't want to return empty-handed. (Yeah, a bit of pride had shown up.)

On top of everything, I wanted to set a good example for Mike. In my early hunting days, I was obsessed with getting meat for the freezer. Now I recognized that the process, not the shooting, is most important. Still, with my wife's great game cooking in mind, I sure hoped we'd get a pronghorn.

As we drove down a dirt road heading toward the northern boundary of our hunting area, a lone buck suddenly came into view. He trotted immediately over a rise toward the southwest more than 500 yards away. *How can he just disappear like that?* I wondered. *These fields are basically flat. Why can't we see him?* We kept looking, but he was gone.

"Maybe he worked his way into the outfitting area," Mike suggested.

We studied the terrain in that area but still didn't see that buck.

Thinking he must have remained somewhere in our area, we continued driving west along the northern boundary. It seemed as if we could see everything in the fields for miles—distant ranches, vehicles, a few trees…but no pronghorn. And we knew at least one was around!

About an hour and a half later, having covered nearly all of our hunting area, I realized there was a strong possibility we were going to get "skunked" and head home without a pronghorn. *Hunting, I reminded myself, is not necessarily finding. So close to pronghorn probably, but our strategies just aren't working. This is the last time I'll hunt during a drought. It sure changes animals' habits. We're done today. At least I saved money by driving the Honda instead of the truck.*

As disappointment tried to set in, I realized our hunt had been successful! Mike and I had time to talk, experience the wide-open fields, and escape from our usual routines and responsibilities.

Not long after he and I turned south to get back to the main highway and head home, we passed a dirt road on the left. Out of curiosity, I stopped, backed up, and drove down the little road. After perhaps 100 yards, the road jogged to the right and then ended. As I looked straight ahead, my jaw dropped. Right in front of us a buck and a doe were standing on a slope hidden from view of anyone driving on the main section roads.

Startled, I hit the brakes and got out slowly, expecting the pronghorn to bolt north. They didn't. I got my rifle, dropped to a prone position in the damp mud, shot once, and missed. *How did I miss?* I pondered, working the bolt on my Ruger 77 .243. Both pronghorn ran perhaps 40 yards and then paused to look at us curiously. This time, my scope brought the doe's image into even clearer focus, I made sure to squeeze the trigger gently but firmly. My bullet traveled the 325 yards and connected with an audible *thump*, but the doe remained standing, her head lowered. Perplexed, the buck remained as if to say, "Hey, let's get going! Why aren't you coming?"

I shot again and down went the doe.

"You hit her again!" Mike exclaimed, getting out of the Honda.

We walked up to her slowly, knowing she could suddenly stand up and run if she'd just been slightly wounded. But she didn't. Even after years of hunting, my heart still pounded with excitement.

Never having watched anyone field dress an animal, Mike held a hind leg and observed everything I did. I was careful to point out the parts to avoid cutting because they would taint the meat. Fifteen minutes later we tied the pronghorn onto the box cart, and pulled it to the car. Moments later Mike slid the doe onto a tarp in the trunk. (Another benefit of hunting with a "young buck" who relishes the opportunity to successfully move a large, dead animal from one place to another. I used to have that desire, but it's been tempered by so many hauling expeditions.)

After stopping to thank both landowners, Mike and I headed home. My thoughts gently convicted me. *A hunter never knows when a strategy that seems not to be working will be successful. If I keep doing what I believe is best to do—the things that have paid off in the past—sooner or later shooting opportunities will arise.*

The relationship Mike and I have deepened as a result of that hunt. During the drive home, we excitedly discussed what we'd seen and how, right at the end, God had surprised us with his provision. Many years ago, an army commander for the king of Aram learned this lesson too. The story is found in the biblical book of 2 Kings, chapter 5.

Naaman, who had leprosy (a skin disease) heard that a prophet of God named Elisha could heal him. So the commander gathered approximately 750 pounds of silver, 150 pounds of gold, and 10 sets of clothing to take with him. The king of Aram wrote this note to the king of Israel: "With this letter I am sending my servant Naaman to you so that you may cure him of his leprosy."

So Naaman and his entourage took off and before long Naaman gave the king of Israel the note from the king of Aram.

As soon as he read the note, the king of Israel became very upset and tore his robes. "Am I God? Can I kill and bring back to life?" he exclaimed. "Why does this fellow send someone to me to be cured of his leprosy? See how he is trying to pick a quarrel with me!"

But there's more to the story.

"When Elisha the man of God heard that the king of Israel had torn his robes, he sent him this message: 'Why have you torn your robes? Have the man come to me and he will know that there is a prophet in Israel.'"

Can you imagine Naaman, along with his servants and soldiers, thundering up to Elisha's front door in their horse-driven chariots?

See the dust?

Hear the snorting horses?

When Naaman's presence was announced at the house, Elisha didn't even come to the door! Instead, he sent a messenger to tell the commander, "Go, wash yourself seven times in the Jordan [River], and your flesh will be restored and you will be cleansed."

Did Naaman laugh and thank the messenger? Did he give the messenger the precious metals and clothing he'd brought? Did he have a feast prepared for everybody in Elisha's neighborhood? No! Naaman was surprised, furious, and indignant. "I thought that [Elisha] would surely come out to me and stand and call on the name of the LORD his God, wave his hand over the spot and cure me of my leprosy." He said to his servants, "Are not Abana and Pharpar, the rivers of Damascus, better than all the waters of Israel? Couldn't I wash in them and be cleansed?"

Fortunately Naaman's servants gave him a dose of common sense and encouraged him to do what Elisha had commanded. So the proud commander relented, went and dipped himself in the Jordan seven times as required, and his skin was healed.

Isn't this a great story? Naaman reminds me of myself. When a problem arises, it's easy for me to ask God for help. No problem. But then I want to legislate how he will fix it. If his actions don't fit my formula, I can become frustrated and angry. God hasn't responded how I'd hoped he'd respond. As with Naaman's problem, sometimes God's solutions are simple. Sometimes they're not.

God loves to surprise us with blessings when we step out in faith believing his promises. Certainly those pronghorn on that little hill surprised Mike and me after we'd developed enough hopeful faith to drive down that one last little road.

If you're an experienced hunter, the next time you go out why not take a new hunter with you who will discover the joys and excitement of hunting? The memories you create may be priceless. And you just might have another willing set of hands and feet to help you get your prize from the field into your freezer!

# 10

# Almost

I'm not a great tracker. I'm probably not as good at tracking as you or your friends might be. My excuse is that I grew up in a suburb of Chicago, where about the only game I could sneak up on were chipmunks, rabbits, squirrels, city-smart deer, and pheasants.

Despite that background, I surprise myself sometimes and get lucky tracking. On one such occasion, two buddies and I were driving from hunting camp into town to grab dinner and get away from our cramped tent and the very cold temperatures. Suddenly six elk ran across the road right in front of us and headed into the dark timber in the national forest. One of them was a huge, six-point bull (that's 12 points for you Easterners).

Five inches of new snow had fallen that morning, so a crazy idea flashed into my mind: *Come here early tomorrow morning, find that bull, and shoot him!* Rather than calculating the odds of actually finding him or realizing that I was so tired I may have been hallucinating, I decided to try.

At sunrise the next morning, I found the spot and followed the elk's trail. At first it was easy because the animals funneled through a narrow ravine heading uphill. Toward the top of the ridge, though, their tracks crisscrossed slightly older tracks of deer and elk.

I'd find "my" elk's tracks...lose them...and find them again. (It was harder than trying to locate a pen on my messy desk!) After nearly two hours, I hit the jackpot—steaming sign. I didn't have to smell it, crush it between my fingers, or put it in a bottle and send it to a laboratory for analysis.

Following the elk sign and tracks, I discovered where they'd bedded down. As adrenaline surged through me, the joy and amazement were almost more than I could handle. (Wouldn't it be great if we could bottle emotions like that to open up and savor later?)

Then I spotted the herd on a hillside, walking slowly approximately 700 yards away from me. That bull was still huge! I knew it would be reckless to try to shoot him at that distance, so I started moving wide to the right to work my way above them.

As I took my first eager steps, a hunter more than 1000 yards away saw those elk and took a "hail Mary" shot.

He missed.

The elk immediately ran up and over the next ridge—and perhaps all the way to another state. There I stood, shaking my head angrily and wishing such hunters would stay around their camp-fires eating donuts all day.

On one hand, I was delighted that I'd tracked those elk so well. That certainly boosted my self-confidence. And I certainly explored beautiful country and pushed myself physically. Yet as I walked back to the road, I felt really disappointed. The end result I'd hoped for—standing next to a huge bull elk I'd shot and wondering how on earth I would get that beast down to the road without horses—didn't happen.

Disappointment on steroids.

*Almost* enough to cause me to give up.

It's awesome how much I can learn from experiences—especially difficult ones—if I give myself the opportunity to look beyond the disappointments and *choose to keep walking* with determination and wisdom on the path God puts ahead of me. For example, what kind of an attitude will I choose to have when...

- I'm deep in the woods and have forgotten my extra ammo and compass?
- the weather worsens rapidly just when I'm in a great spot and 15 minutes of shooting light remain?
- I've done award-winning crawl strokes over 100 yards of rock and cactus—and then missed a 100-yard shot at a grazing animal because I didn't load a round into the chamber after I left the tent at five o'clock that morning? *Click!*

Reflecting on my hunting adventures and misadventures, I realize how much my attitude influences my hunting and many other areas of life. Perhaps my best lesson concerning disappointment and attitude came from a hunter in his mid-thirties who was camped next to us along a river in minus 40-degree weather. He accidentally drove his Scout II off a snowy wilderness road and landed in a snow-covered pond. He then rode out on the back of his brother's ATV for an hour to get to camp. When we met up, he told me simply, "My day wasn't all that great."

What keeps people trying...instead of surrendering?

Experimenting instead of rusting away in boredom?

Pushing limits when we could be lifting sodas or ice cream spoons?

Smiling (at least on the outside) instead of cussing?

Remaining good-natured when friends or spouses see us after a hunting adventure and ask, "Get anything?" and we have to answer *no*?

I like these bits of ancient wisdom found in the book of Proverbs:

> A happy heart makes the face cheerful, but heartache crushes the spirit (15:13).

> All the days of the oppressed are wretched, but the cheerful heart has a continual feast (15:15).

Sometimes I've felt like giving up. I've wondered if my legs could take another step…or if there were any pheasants, deer, rabbits, elk, coyotes…within five miles of me.

Sometimes I've spent time in camp sipping coffee and getting an attitude adjustment.

Sometimes I wish I could laugh at myself more often.

After particularly challenging hunting trips, I've returned home to face even more attitude challenges:

- I struggled to cross the creek of pain when two discs in my back rebelled with agonizing consequences.

- My feet dragged through emotional mud when I thought about visiting my handicapped, schizophrenic sister yet again and seeing her blinded eye and crippled hand caused by a deranged man.

- The sleet of confusion blinded me, and I lost sight of God's love and enduring truths. I wanted to find a tree-stand overlooking a just-harvested cornfield and remain there forever.

- I longed for a "camp day" so I wouldn't have to review a mountain of paperwork—mostly bills—needing immediate attention.

- I wanted to hit the "redo this part of life" button and check out mentally, spiritually, emotionally, and physically when my marriage hit a rocky spot.

- Old memories and wrongdoing have struck my spirit like wind-driven hailstones.

- My faith in God has been tested by tornado-force doubts.

- My faults have jumped out at me like the striking rattlesnake I killed while on a pronghorn hunt.

I hope I'm not the only hunter who faces challenges like these while negotiating the paths of life. Fortunately I can cling to the refreshing and encouraging truths of God's promises found in the Bible. I know that the best Guide in the universe—who is also skilled in desert wanderings—is with me during the easy times and the "where in the heck is some water and shade" wilderness times.

God shows me that his compass always points toward spending eternity with him in heaven.

He reminds me of his unfolding plans for my life.

He sloshes living water over my sweaty face.

He challenges me to go wherever he leads.

And he promises to provide whatever I need in order to follow him obediently.

# Freedom to Thrive

Standing on the cattle guard, I undid the lock and opened the gate so my hunting buddies and I could enter the 10,000-acre ranch. We were the only hunters allowed on the property! As the setting October sun created ever-lengthening shadows on the fields, my anticipation level was off the scales. We quickly set up camp near a decaying ranch house. At one time it was the hub of family and work life. Now sections of the roof were exposed to bare wood, the steps were rotten, and pigeons flew in and out of an upstairs window.

We piled into the Jeep to do some scouting, heading east on a dirt road toward a large, fenced pasture and one of several watering troughs filled by a windmill pump. As I admired the country, I thought about the odd course of events that enabled us to hunt here.

We'd wanted to hunt this land for several years, and we'd heard that the ranch manager decided which hunters he'd let on the property and which ones he wouldn't. Soon after we met him at the ranch headquarters to ask for permission, he announced the words we'd dreaded. "Nope. You guys can't hunt here. Find another spot."

We were disappointed, but we didn't give up. Hoping he'd change his mind, we talked to him several more times before hunting seasons with no success. We later learned the only way to gain permission was to buy him a case of expensive whiskey or give him an expensive rifle, which wasn't something we felt comfortable doing.

When we heard a new ranch manager had been hired, we stopped by to talk to him. He granted us permission as soon as he heard our story. "Anybody the former manager let on," he stated, "won't hunt anywhere on our ranches. You're just the type of hunters we want."

In the seven years since then, we'd hunted this property and learned where the pronghorn traveled. They often moved from the huge, mostly flat land to the south through an area of gullies and dips to the higher third of the ranch to the north. We'd studied where the placements of fenceposts and water tanks would allow us to sneak up on these alert animals grazing hundreds of yards away.

Now we were driving down dirt roads hoping to find pronghorn and be able to determine where they might be when first light came tomorrow, opening day of hunting season. In many respects, these antelope-like creatures had the upper hand—binocular vision, incredible speed, knowledge of predators that seemed to be passed from generation to generation. (No wonder they'd run full speed onto posted "no hunting" property as soon as the first rifle shot echoed from a faraway field.)

I wanted to shoot my first buck on the first day of hunting season. I was so excited about experiencing that rush of adrenaline! I envisioned trying to relax and breathe slowly while squeezing the trigger of my .243. Conversely, I also wanted the hunt to last for days for the sheer joy of doing what I love in such a beautiful place. But with unusual daytime temperatures rising into the sixties, I knew any downed animal would need to be processed fairly quickly, which would require heading home soon or packing it on ice.

Have you felt this way? Trying to strategize in order to locate and shoot the selected animals—and yet hoping that the best strategies might require days of hard-but-enjoyable effort before filling a tag? Then you know how I felt as we drove through several miles of pastureland. When we rounded the top of a small hill, we stopped. Five hundred yards away and perhaps that same distance from the main highway, a herd of pronghorn—some bedded down, some standing—watched us watch them.

We got out of the Jeep, a cool west wind at our backs, and focused our conversation on two topics: how far the herd might travel overnight and how big the herd buck was. It was by far the biggest buck we'd seen on this ranch. Rather than disturbing them further, we hopped back into the Jeep and returned to camp. Over a lasagna dinner (the kind that's already prepared and just needs heating), bread, and veggies, we determined our strategies.

My father-in-law, Roy, opted to sit inside a dry water tank about a mile away. He planned to be there as the sun came up.

Walt, another hunting buddy, agreed to drop Roy off and then position himself inside an abandoned building south of the herd we'd just seen.

I opted to ride with Walt for a while and then hop out just east of where we'd seen the herd. Several small hills there would afford me cover. I planned to try a new strategy—to use the bright, rising sun behind me to momentarily blind any pronghorn that looked my way. That would hide my stalking and hopefully allow me to get within shooting range of that buck.

"That's a great idea," my buddies said. "Sounds as if it'll work."

Full of food and exciting thoughts, I climbed into bed and hoped my father-in-law wouldn't snore too loudly. Turns out he did, but the earplugs I brought quickly solved that problem. Hunting regularly together, the three of us had learned through the years to bring earplugs and several clocks so we wouldn't sleep through the alarms. We set them to go off early enough to give us time to get ready, eat a warm cereal breakfast, and consume some energy drinks. We never know how far our hunting might take us or when we might get back to camp so we always eat at least a little breakfast and pack lunches to give us the energy we need to hunt all day.

Opening morning, after our usual morning routine, we headed

out. Squeezing rifles and ammo, water for pronghorn gut-washing, tarps, other necessary equipment, and ourselves into the Jeep, off we went. The sun was just starting to come up, and we knew we should have left camp 30 minutes earlier. Ten minutes later, Roy was setting up in the water tank. As we moved on, I eagerly scanned the fields for pronghorn. I saw one and then another.

"Get out here," Walt suggested, "and I'll keep driving." (Pronghorn are very curious, and they love to watch a moving vehicle. When it stops, they'll often run away, having learned that loud noises and danger often occur after a vehicle quits moving. That's why hunting drivers slow way down to drop off hunters on the side opposite pronghorn. They want to keep the vehicle moving.)

The next half hour is etched into my memory. I walked over the first low hill, knowing I had one more hill between me and the buck. I removed the scope caps and kept walking. With the brilliant, orange sun behind me, I dropped down and crept to the crest of the next hill and peeked over. The herd hadn't spooked, and the big buck was chasing his does around playfully. He'd run around one side, moving the herd a little bit, and then he'd shift position and chase a doe the other way.

*How am I going to get a shot?* I mused. *They're nearly 500 yards away, and even using my bipod that's a long shot.* I slowly moved closer on all fours, making sure I kept dirt out of the muzzle and avoided intimate encounters with cactus spines. I'd never tried to use the sun in a specific strategy like this before. I hoped if the buck did see my movement, since he'd be looking directly into the sun he wouldn't recognize I was a danger. From time to time I watched the herd through my binoculars, trying to figure out where the pronghorn might move next—hopefully a bit closer to me.

Suddenly the buck stopped and stared right at me.

I froze. *How'd he spot me since he had to stare right into the sun?* I wondered.

The huge buck trotted toward me—a move I hadn't expected.

*Where'll I go now? I can't go back over the top of the hill, and I only have a few low places in front of me.* I scooted into a small depression and dropped into my favorite prone shooting position. I kept my head down and out of sight. My mind started buzzing with *what ifs.* What if he doesn't come this far? What if he decides to circle this hill and come up behind me? What if he turns around and moves the herd farther away?

My best option seemed to be remaining where I was—ready to shoot and hoping the buck maintained enough interest in me to keep coming all the way across the field and up part of the hill.

Fifteen seconds passed.

Another 30 seconds passed.

I lifted my head a bit. Suddenly I could see his head. He stopped, moved his head from side to side, and stared at me for perhaps 30 seconds. He took several steps closer, and more of his body appeared.

Fortunately I was looking at him through my scope.

*Now he's too close!* I realized. *I'd bet-ter aim low because of the bullet's arc… but not too low.*

The buck disappeared from view momentarily, evidently going into a small dip I couldn't see. When I saw him again he was closer and much higher. He was amazing! His horns were at least 12 inches long!

His eyes fixed on me—a shape he knew wasn't supposed to be here. Now 75 yards away, he stopped again. I aimed for a point low on his chest and squeezed. The immediate thunk told me it was a good hit, and he dropped in his tracks.

The plains and hills around me were silent as I rose and walked slowly to him. As I gazed down at him, I was thankful for the provision of meat he'd provide. I also decided to see if my wife and I had enough money in reserve to have a taxidermist mount his magnificent head.

I was excited about how this new strategy had worked and smiled at the unexpected aspects of it, including the buck walking toward me to figure out what I was. I considered how thoughtful it was for my hunting buddies to encourage me to try this new approach.

In the process of encouraging me to try the "sun strategy," my buddies ministered to me more than they know. In fact, later on I took their example and applied it to one of my blind spots.

I've had many opportunities to influence my daughter's life, including participating in some of her major experiences—first camping trip, first day at school, first fishing trip, first target shooting, first ride on a snowboard, first softball game, first day at college. And, I'm sorry to say, at times I probably held her back from experiencing other adventures she might have enjoyed. Sometimes, for example, I chose to work rather than take time off to do fun things with her.

Now that my daughter is older, I hope I'm a little wiser. I'm trying to find a healthy balance between encouraging her to try new things on her own and asking her to try things I enjoy. Although I can explain how and why I do things a certain way, I need to be careful not to exert unnecessary (and perhaps harmful) pressure on her to do things the way I might want them done.

I've determined that the best help I can provide for Caitlin now that she's a young adult is spiritual guidance. I strive to encourage her to keep allowing God's love and truth to permeate her life. After all, he is the one with the big picture in mind. When the rocky paths of life come—and come they will—he is the strategy expert. He is faithful in guiding people toward complete trust in him. I'm thankful for that.

Come to think about it, maybe it's time to thank my hunting buddies for how they encouraged me to go after that buck and let them know it impacted more than my hunting ability.

# Lost

I sweated drops of fear-laden moisture as I stood under a large pine tree—and for good reason. I'd really blown it.

As Roy and I slid down the steep, icy road into the valley only minutes earlier, I'd rationalized that my two-wheel-drive truck with tire chains would surely get us back up. Enthusiasm had flooded my system with artificial certainty. *This is the place…the moment… when I'll get my deer.*

Suddenly seven deer crossed the edge of a meadow 200 yards away. In record time, I stopped the truck, removed my rifle from its case, and loaded it.

"I'll be right back," I promised Roy. (The next time I get a feeling like that, I hope I'm at home near my woodstove with a cup of coffee in my hand and my leg chained to a recliner.)

As I stepped through 10 inches of snow, I didn't pay much attention to dark clouds racing south or the snowflakes swirling all around me. Yes, a mental red flag popped up: *Snow is coming!* But my pressing agenda shoved the thought away and drove me on.

Oh, did I forget to mention that I left my loaded-for-bear pack in the truck? Eager anticipation and rationalization pushed aside years of experience and common sense as I followed the steaming deer sign. *I'm only going a little ways, so why go back and get the pack? When I get the deer, I'll return and get what I need.* I picked up my pace. *I've hunted enough that I can adapt to any situation.*

Wind stung my cheeks and blew snow into my boot prints. I briskly climbed a ridge as I tracked the deer into even denser timber. After 10 minutes or so, sweat stuck my cotton T-shirt to my chest like a magnet on a refrigerator door.

Encouraged by more fresh sign, I walked even faster.

*I'd better slow down and zip open my jacket a little to let some heat out so I don't get chilled.* But I had places to go and a deer to shoot so I kept on.

*It'll be great when I return to get the sled to haul my deer!* Pride was already giving me a shooting award in front of an audience of one.

When I realized the deer had changed direction, going north instead of west, and that I'd never catch up to them, reality hit.

*This is not good!* I experienced the same fear I'd felt in India when a flood almost swept the taxi I was in down into a gorge. (The car began to float!) I'd felt the same dizzying rush on a roller-coaster ride when my body twisted and turned just before I got sick and made the ride attendant angry.

I knew what to do:

- admit I was lost
- stop walking
- inventory my resources
- make and implement a strategic plan

I had a small Swiss Army knife, layers of clothing (although the inner ones were sweat-soaked), my rifle, ammo, a few matches, and 10 feet of parachute cord. I also had plenty of goose bumps. I sure was missing my tube tent, ripstop nylon tarp, food, a pot for boiling water, fire starter, raincoat, water, flashlight, and toilet paper. They were all in my daypack.

I bet you know what I did.

Did I apply skills gleaned from years of outdoor activities and survival books? No. I thought, *I'll figure out where I am and get back to the truck eventually. No problem.* So I started walking…a blind man leading himself. Then I saw *them.* Not deer. Not a small Forest Service cabin with a sign reading "Lost Hunter Enter Here." Not hunters sitting near a popping fire with hot chocolate in hand. What did I see? My size 14-D boot prints.

As if on cue, snow fell more heavily and the wind picked up. Finally the right message flattened me. *I am lost, and I have barely enough to survive a night of deep snow and bitter cold. I can create a shelter and get a fire going. I'm rapidly running out of options—and daylight.*

Have you ever ignored warning signs? Disregarded the truth and gave in to the emotions of the moment? Gave way to being macho? Tried to escape the basic laws of life and the resulting consequences from breaking them? Are these rationalizations familiar? (Feel free to add your own.)

- It's okay for me to study with that attractive woman at her apartment. She needs my help to get her degree.

- I can pad my expense account a little. Who will know?

- I have a right to remain angry toward my wife. She started the argument.

- My son will understand if I'm late for his football game. The money I'm making by closing this deal will help him go to college.

Suddenly dense-timber stillness surprised me. The wind lessened. I thought I could actually hear snowflakes landing on the ground—lots of them! Before I started to make my pine-bough shelter or snow cave, find dry wood, and hunt for something edible, I did the only thing I knew to do before kicking into pure survival mode.

"Hello! Roy, can you hear me?" I yelled. Then I stopped and listened.

A faint "Hello!" from Roy echoed in the valley.

Joy swept through me.

Yelling back and forth, Roy and I finally met in the woods. I discovered that at one point I'd been within 15 feet of a narrow road that would have led me to the truck. Sitting in the warm truck once again, relief flooded me. One lesson I learned while I was lost etched itself into the fiber of my being: *It's easy to ignore warning signs and go full speed ahead.*

Are you familiar with some of these warnings?

- "I'm your body. Get to the gym *now*."
- "I'm your friend. Stop showing me the you that you want me to see. Let me see the *real* you."
- "I'm your wife. Please spend time with me—and not just when you want something."
- "I'm your child. I need you to help me figure out this male/female relationship stuff."
- "I'm your conscience. You need to ask that person for forgiveness because you were selfish."
- "I'm God, and my Word is truth. Please love me with all your heart, all your soul, all your mind, and all your strength. And love your neighbor as yourself."
- "I'm your spirit. You need to laugh and enjoy life more."

Take it from a guy who has blown it. Calling out for help sure beats walking around in circles. And God always answers the cries of his people. Sometimes he replies in a gentle whisper (1 Kings 19:12-15). Sometimes he uses a blast of freezing sleet across our faces. What are some of the things he says?

"Yes."

"No."

"Wait."

"Are you serious?"

Many years ago, God gave a guy an opportunity to take steps of faith so we can learn from his story. Let's picture ourselves near him and track the clues regarding his identity.

- He lives in a country with no navy—only small boats.
- He has little if any money and no pension plan.
- His clothes likely came from a local thrift shop.
- He receives money from passersby after using his usually hoarse voice and gestures to manipulate them.
- His words are always variations on the same theme: "Give me some money because I need a little food. Any bit will do. Have pity on me."
- He's blind and has no health insurance plan despite serious health problems.

Do you know who he is? His name is Bartimaeus, the son of Timaeus (Mark 10:46-52). Normally we don't read about a guy who moves from the gutter to center stage literally. Only seven Bible verses describe this scene. Let's picture it together.

Bartimaeus sits by the roadside at Jericho and begs. Perhaps his extended family is fed up with his complaints, his awkward tumbles, his need to eat while doing nothing to bring in copper coins. So maybe they put him out on the streets and tried to assuage their guilt. We don't know.

This guy could probably write a scroll titled *The Art of Begging in Ten Easy Steps*. He was trapped in darkness and depressive thoughts. He had no hope for the future. And he was quite literally lost in the crowds. I'm sure Bartimaeus felt insignificant, alone, lonely...lost.

Jesus leaves Jericho, a bustling city long since rebuilt after God broke down its walls shortly after the Israelites entered Canaan (renamed Israel) (Joshua 6:1-20; 1 Kings 16:34). Crowds of people tag along. It's a parade without a festival, a welcomed change from the ordinary.

Jesus does miracles some say only God can do. He teaches the Torah and Jewish laws so well that listeners are amazed. He acts so very different from other rabbis and religious leaders—including the popular and influential ones.

Bartimaeus' attention perks up. Instead of begging, he listens. Jesus is nearby. Mustering all the air his dust-filled lungs can hold, he yells out this request: "Jesus, Son of David, have mercy on me!" This blind man understands ancestral lineage and admits he needs mercy—unmerited favor.

"Be quiet!" irritated celebrants yell. This guy is ruining the ambiance.

Again and again Bartimaeus hollers out the same eight words. He longs for mercy. For the Master's voice or touch. For recognition that he means something to someone. For healing.

Jesus stops. "Call him," he commands, focusing attention on this deeply wounded, "trying not to hope but is unable to stifle it" guy.

"Cheer up!" bystanders tell Bartimaeus. "On your feet! He's calling you."

Jesus offers Bartimaeus a new direction that requires a new faith. And he does the same for us.

Bartimaeus could stay in his favorite begging spot. Continue to trust in people's fickle generosity. Exercise his manipulative voice and time-proven hand gestures more creatively. But he doesn't. He throws his cloak aside, jumps up, and hurries to Jesus. (I'm guessing he knocks people over in the process.) Perhaps he's thinking, *Nothing will get in my way! Jesus heard my cries! He wants me to come to him! I matter.*

Something strange happens next. Jesus asks him, "What do you want me to do for you?"

"Isn't that obvious?" we think.

But Bartimaeus doesn't question it. He just answers.

"Rabbi, I want to see!" Hope floods the reservoir of Bartimaeus' empty, needy, unloved heart.

"Go!" Jesus says next. "Your faith has healed you."

Wait a minute! God, in the person of Jesus, just healed this man's eyes, right? Yes. And he used steps of faith as the catalyst.

Bartimaeus doesn't debate Jesus' divinity or question whether or not Jesus can heal blind eyes.

Bartimaeus doesn't respond sarcastically, "Why else would I hurry over here—to say hello?"

No!

He shouts out for mercy. And he receives it from the one who came to earth to make the ultimate sacrifice of mercy—to be crucified for all humanity's sins.

What can we take away from Bartimaeus' experience? Well, how might our lives be different if we…

- honestly evaluate our needs and our helplessness?

- realize we need heavenly help rather than trying to handle difficult things ourselves?

- call out to God, asking for his mercy, and then do what he tells us to do?

I'm sure it would be humbling. It would upset our equilibrium—especially our sinful habits, sinful attitudes, false presuppositions, and any part of our foundations built on sand. It would require faith and believing God's promises presented in his Word. Consider these teachings by Jesus:

- Do not worry, saying, "What shall we eat?" or "What shall we drink?" or "What shall we wear?" For the pagans run after all these things, and your heavenly Father knows that you need them. But seek first his kingdom

and his righteousness, and all these things will be given
to you as well (Matthew 6:31-33).

- If any of you lacks wisdom, you should ask God, who
  gives generously to all without finding fault, and it will
  be given to him (James 1:5).

- I have told you these things, so that in me you may have
  peace. In this world you will have trouble. But take heart!
  I have overcome the world (John 16:33).

Yes, we'll certainly face challenges no matter how we approach
Jesus. Maybe *crawling* through past pain. Maybe *kneeling* in repen-
tance. Maybe *calling out* in a crowded-but-lonely room. Maybe hes-
itantly *taking small steps* through the minefield of addiction. Maybe
*leaping* toward the Light of the World who loves us and wants all of
us to choose him so he can take us out of spiritual darkness.

We'll hear jeers. Face doubts. Have to expand the listening skills
of our minds and hearts in order to join God in what he desires to
do in and through us as he carries out his plans and purposes.

Our faith steps toward Jesus will always lead to blessings—in this
life and in the life to come. Jesus guarantees it.

Are you ready to receive kingdom eyes—a new way of seeing life?
A new matrix of understanding? I urge you to meet God in a fresh or
new way. He is calling you! He delights in helping lost people.

Even those who do not yet realize they are lost.

# 13

# Hopes and Risks

This morning when I walked with my German Shepherd, it was 0 degrees F., which is higher than it has been. My cold ears immediately reminded me of an unforgettable adventure near Gunnison, Colorado, during a late-season elk hunt.

As you know, we hunters are among the most hope-filled people on earth. We devote great amounts of time and resources to fulfilling our hopes of getting out into God's country; tromping through marshes, poison ivy, and bug-infested woods; and exploring types of terrain even a coon dog might avoid. Why? In order to slip on ice, get *really* cold feet, sweat, become "micro lost," slap mosquitoes, and possibly bag wild pigs, pheasants, quail, deer, elk, ducks, geese, pronghorn, bear…and other game animals too numerous to list.

Certainly hope filled my mind when I discovered a unique opportunity to be in a special drawing for a December elk hunt. I talked my two friends into applying too, and we waited expectantly to discover if we'd been chosen. When my tag arrived in the mail, I could hardly contain my excitement. I checked with my two friends, and they got tags too. Yep, we'd be hunting elk near their wintering area. With a season that late, surely they'd have migrated from the surrounding high-country wilderness.

I first prepared my old, three-season cabover camper to make sure everything worked. Then I did the same thing to my Ford pickup, which might qualify for "classic license plate" status by age only—or by recognition that the only kind of "show" classic my truck would qualify for is a no show. Its rust spots, muffler noises, and small trail of exhaust smoke from tired cylinder rings provide its own status. It would carry the heavy cabover.

*I sure hope this hunt is memorable,* I thought. *It's time we got into a herd of elk and limited out.* Our recent elk hunts had been difficult because the animals were remaining inaccessibly high up in the mountains. Even people packing in to the backcountry with horses got skunked.

The day before opening day, the three of us headed west in our vehicles and found a beautiful campsite along the Gunnison River. Set in a picturesque valley, the water gurgling 25 feet away sounded great. I should have paid more attention to the amount of ice in the water, however.

We knew it would be cold and had prepared, we thought, for all eventualities. I had five bottles of propane for the heater and stove in the cabover, and my wife had packed plenty of great food knowing how much three cold, hungry hunters can eat. Walt and I each had .30-06 rifles with 180-grain bullets. Roy was carrying a .300 Win mag.

Our first day we chained up the Jeep and drove about 15 minutes to reach our hunting area. At one spot, seven hunters sat in their vehicles observing a huge meadow below dark timber—a dense forest with thick underbrush. We were sure all of them had heaters going full blast. We stopped, rolled down our windows, and talked with a few of them.

"We sit and wait," one guy told me, his breath making vapor trails out of his truck window, "until the elk cross the meadow."

Staying in our heated vehicle sounded good to us, yet we were still crazy enough to get out to find elk. *Besides,* I wondered, *with that many hunters in one spot, who's to say who shot which animal if a herd does come out?*

We forged ahead, four-wheeling up a steep hill covered with snow, ice, and big rocks. Then we parked and split up. Roy investigated a small, tree-covered area to the left on the edge of the ridge. Walt and I explored in other directions. We saw many elk tracks, which gave us hope that we could figure out the elk's patterns—where they bedded down, where they found grass and water, and where they took photographs of hunters looking for them.

I believed this would be one of our best hunts ever!

But I kept making a slight miscalculation. I didn't listen to a weather forecast.

May I make a confession before describing anything else? I always enjoy eating chips—especially Fritos—and small chocolate bars while hunting in cold weather. I rationalize this by thinking, *This will keep my calories up and my energy going strong.* Through the years, I've probably consumed 20,000 more calories than most people would burn off. Thankfully, as I've mentioned, I've been blessed with a tall, lanky frame. Anyway, this trip was no exception to my snack rules. And did that junk food taste great!

We hunted outside much of the day as the temperature dropped. In the early evening, we gladly entered the cabover to eat a "one pot" meal. For those of you who are unfamiliar with this term, it's a fancy phrase describing a large, cast-iron pot into which the designated cook piles (oops—combines) meat with cans of veggies and maybe soup and seasonings. Adding to this, we ate about a third of a loaf of buttered bread, sipped apple cider, and finished up with my version of a camp pie. I took some buttered bread and added pie filling on top. Using a little cooker, I heated the bread with filling until the toast was browned. Delicious!

That night we all got cold because the temperature dipped below zero, and the little heater couldn't even get the temperature up to 40 degrees. As soon as I woke up, not wanting a mutiny on my hands, I turned on a supplementary, stand-alone propane heater—the kind you're not supposed to use indoors. (Since the cabover leaks so much air, I didn't worry about the gas fumes.)

The next two days while hunting we changed a few things:

- We broadened our search area.
- I slipped on an icy hill, chose to drop down to my knees on the rocky ground instead of falling backward, and cracked a bone in my right leg.
- The temperature would get up to -10 degrees F. each day.
- We shivered more during our shorter excursions.
- We ran the heater in the Jeep at top speed and even used the fancy seat heaters.
- We found ourselves walking even faster during our brief hunting forays.

We kept glassing the meadows and forest carefully, studying elk tracks along the roads to see where they crossed and in which directions. Sometimes we worked sections of dark timber as a team, trying to drive elk out of their beds. (This occurred fewer and fewer times as our noses, fingers, and ears grew redder and redder and we got smarter and smarter.) We weren't prepared for this kind of cold that dropped down to -25 degrees—not counting the wind chill factor. My mustache got so icy I was afraid it might break off.

On the third evening when we reached the cabover, we couldn't get in! The lock had frozen solid. Finally acting as wise adults rather than hope-filled, frozen hunters, we spent that night in a 72-degree motel room. We were sure glad because the temperature, along with the wind chill factor, dipped to -50 degrees!

The next morning, we somewhat reluctantly put on our gear and let the vehicle warm up completely before heading out (keep this a secret; don't want to blow our image). I purchased a spray that would melt the ice in the cabover lock, and we drove to the campsite. When I opened the cabover door, we discovered that everything inside had frozen solid—water, cans of food, leather boots, and underwear. The cabover heater kept stopping because after the top fifth of propane in a tank was used, the tank would no longer work. (A hunter with an engineering bent later explained to me in detail why this occurred, but I only remember that "it was just too cold for even propane heaters to work.")

We didn't see any elk that fourth afternoon, yet each of us expressed gratefulness for the opportunity to be out there. Experiencing the beauty of God's creation. Being thankful for long johns. Still running the heater in the Jeep full blast. Eating chocolate bars and chips. We also discussed the risks of hunting in such incredibly cold temperatures. We could no longer hike outside for hours, even though we wore layers of clothing. The risk of frostbite was too great.

The last morning before we needed to leave, we drove down snow-covered roads, tire chains rumbling—expectantly hoping to see elk standing next to the road wearing signs that read: "Here I am, cold and tired. End my misery please, and put parts of me in a warm, cast-iron skillet." That didn't happen.

*What if we get several elk?* I thought. *How are we going to deal with them in this cold?* I discovered part of the answer several hours later.

About two o'clock, I noticed through my binoculars something dark and moving. A large herd of elk was crossing a hill to our east and running right toward us!

"Hey," I said profoundly, "I see some. Right over there—coming this way!"

We headed toward them.

My heart was racing with anticipation. *Finally we'll get our chance!* We drove several hundred yards to the base of a hill. I couldn't see the elk, but I knew they'd keep coming unless a hunter shot at them, the herd bull suddenly got wiser, or a vehicle with hunters pulled in front of them. "Drop me off right here, please," I stated. "I'll get out and wait for them. What do you both want to do?" They chose to remain in the vehicle a bit longer and parked about 80 yards away.

*In just a few minutes,* I reasoned, *elk will gallop right over the top of this hill.* No matter how many times I hunt, I always get nervous in situations like this. *Where should I position myself? If they go to the left side of the hill or to the right, where can I safely shoot so my bullets don't end up flying across the plains and hitting who knows what? Will I lead the elk just right so I can hit it? Should I stand up or sit to shoot?*

I climbed into the ditch by the road, sinking up past my knees in the snow, and headed uphill about 10 yards and knelt by a large patch of sage. I wanted to be sure I had good "shooting windows" above and to each side while remaining at least partially hidden.

I waited impatiently for the elk. Time slowed down. I focused my gaze intently on the top of the hill, hoping I wouldn't fog up a lens on my scope or my glasses. I remembered how quickly bullets drop when fired in such cold temperatures.

Suddenly bobbing elk heads appeared, and then the rest of their bodies. The first 10 stampeded over the top of the hill, legs crunching, bodies melding into a brown mass. I selected a large cow near the head of the herd and fired. Immediately a cloud of snow flew up, and the herd shifted to my right.

I heard my buddies get out of the vehicle. They moved to the other side of the road and shot several times at elk that were heading up a steep slope toward the dark timber.

Keeping an eye on the general area where I'd shot, I decided not to shoot at another elk as the rest of the herd thundered past. Having only one tag, I didn't want two elk down, and I wasn't sure if I'd hit that cow. Then I saw something. I focused on an elk lying on the hillside. *I got my elk!* At that moment, I didn't feel the intense cold or notice how wet my wool pants were. I was just really happy.

Wading through the snow, I approached the elk carefully. I

touched an eye with a sage branch and got no reflex. My bullet had passed near the heart and gone through the lungs. Now the real "fun" started. I walked back to the Jeep to get my pack holding my knife, small bone saw, and other essentials. My cheeks were red, and my fingers were already a bit numb.

"So," Walt asked, "what's the plan? I vote for leaving the elk right where it is, as it is, and dealing with it tomorrow morning."

Knowing we had less than two hours of daylight left, I pondered this. I announced that I'd at least gut the beast that was larger than some horses.

"It's 25 below zero," Walt countered, "too dangerous to be out here. And," he added, "remember that I grew up in Africa. I hate this kind of cold. I'll wait right here in the Jeep."

Realizing that Roy, in his late seventies, shouldn't spend a lot of time breathing such cold air, I headed to the elk alone. *I got an elk!… I sure wish I had help tying back this leg…Sure is cold…Glad we're not too far from the road…Sure is cold!*

Thankfully, heat rising from the elk's cavity, along with the combined four layers of clothing I wore, kept me fairly warm despite increasing wind gusts. But everything took longer than usual. I had to be especially careful to not cut myself on sharp pieces of bone. When I finally finished gutting (sorry: *field dressing*, a funny phrase actually) with fewer than 10 minutes of daylight left, I took off my thin, blood-soaked wool gloves, and they froze immediately! I knew I'd better get back to the vehicle before my fingers did the same thing. Before I left, knowing how much coyotes hate the smell of human urine, I "marked my territory" to keep them away from my hard-earned animal.

The next morning, the Jeep started—thankfully—because the cold by the river was worse than any cold I'd ever experienced. Twenty minutes later, we were dragging the elk down the hill. Roy tied long nylon ropes together, and we used the Jeep to drag the elk in stages the rest of the way to the road through sagebrush and scrub oak. Every part of the elk had frozen solid except for small sections deep inside the hindquarters. *Duh,* I thought, *this has been in a deep freeze all night!*

Despite the cold, I was sweating when we got the elk to the edge of the road and loaded it into my '60s Chevrolet pickup trailer using a come-along and several boards. *Hurray for clothes that wick away moisture!* I thought, moving my numb fingers inside my gloves.

Back at camp, we got everything stowed away. I got the truck started with the help of a fellow hunter who walked up holding a large cup. "When it's this cold," he advised, "you have to pour lots of gas down the carburetor because you can't get enough gas in there by just pumping the pedal. Good thing you have a carburetor." Amazingly, after not being started for days, the old Ford coughed and sputtered to life, and we gratefully left that frigid place.

That night at a motel, I plugged in a little magnetic electric heater and stuck it on the now-warmed oil pan hoping that would help the engine start the next morning. It worked! The truck started after a few coughs, but I couldn't shift. The stick simply moved around the transmission like a spoon in nearly frozen honey. I managed to put the truck in reverse and got it to move a foot. Then I put it in granny low and moved forward a foot. After 40 minutes of going up and back like this, the transmission finally began working. I drove slowly around the block and stopped to get gas.

"How cold is it?" I asked the attendant.

"Well, the temperature plus wind chill puts it 58 degrees below zero," he said. When I told him where we'd camped, he gave me a funny look as if I were dazed, confused, or from another planet. He then added, "The temperature is always lower in the valley by the river."

I didn't know whether to feel macho or stupid.

After we got back home, I hung the elk until it thawed out.

My wife and I ate the cans of food that had frozen.

Walt decided that he would never hunt in -30 degree F. weather again. And even more wisely, he would never sleep during extremely cold weather in a three-season cabover.

Roy, the wise sage, agreed with Walt.

Do you remember how I'd hoped this would be a memorable hunt? Well, it sure was. Be careful what you wish for!

What made that hunt so memorable wasn't the taking of an elk, planning hunting strategies, cracking my bone, mutual shivering, or the enjoyable meals as we talked about life. Rather, it was the go-for-broke risks we faced every day dealing with such bitter cold and how we met those challenges. Our adventure (plus near and actual frostbite) bonded us together like ice cubes in a freezer tray.

Have you considered the role of risk in your life? Many people prefer to try to eliminate risk from their lives or take on only little, easily manageable slices of risk. When we're avoiding or limiting risk...

- we choose hunting spots too close to the road and close to our vehicles.

- we drive far too often and stalk too seldom.

- we wear so much clothing we're like marshmallow men unable to do much of anything.

- we settle for afternoons in motel rooms watching hunting and fishing shows on TV.

That December elk trip pushed me to the max, but I survived. I'm still filled with confident pride every time I think about it. Even so, I still shy away from taking risks sometimes. Especially at home.

I find myself refusing to try a different way to communicate with my wife.

I'm hesitant to spend weeks developing a book proposal on speculation.

I reach a certain point during discussions with men when I want to self-protect, make excuses, and cover up past mistakes rather than being open and vulnerable and waiting to see what happens next.

Sometimes I refuse to step out in faith even though I know God is with me every step of the way.

I pray cautiously sometimes rather than standing in faith and letting God know what I really need, how I'm really feeling, and what miracles I'd like him to do in the lives of family, friends—and my own.

The Bible encourages us by revealing many instances of God blessing people reluctant or unwilling to take risks by "being with them" and providing wisdom, courage, protection, and other things they needed.

- Called by God to be the father of the Israelite nation, Abram left his country and spent the rest of his life as a nomad in unfamiliar territory.

- After Moses died, Joshua, even though he was fearful of the future, agreed to lead the Israelites—former slaves in Egypt—into the promised land because God promised to be with him.

- Gideon, after threshing wheat secretly in a winepress to avoid enemies, finally trusted God enough to obey him. With only 300 soldiers, Gideon routed a huge Midianite army with God's help.

- Barak, chosen by God to destroy the pagan army of the king of Canaan, reluctantly agreed to go fight—but only if God's prophetess Deborah accompanied him. Because of his hedging, Barak defeated the enemy but didn't receive the added blessing of bringing down King Jaban's military commander, Sisera.

- After Jesus spoke to Saul, who had persecuted and killed followers of Jesus, God spoke to Ananias in a vision and told him to help Saul. Objecting at first, Ananias obeyed. Saul, later renamed Paul, used his relationship with Jesus and his knowledge as a rabbi to spread Jesus' message.

I've had times in my life when I didn't risk much...if anything. I liked the safety, feeling as if I could control my circumstances and not wanting to step out on a limb for anybody or any cause. Then circumstances rocked my world and forced me to not only experience risk but to also realize my need to be pushed by risk to draw me closer to God in faith. Sometimes difficult things have drawn me closer to God and forced me to reevaluate personal issues. The death of my cousin. Car accidents. Major surgery. Stock market crash. Job termination. Suicide of a good friend.

What risks have you faced or are facing right now? God calls each of us to risk—to have ongoing adventures. Some are easy; some shake us to the core of our being. What risks might you willingly undertake? Here are a few ideas to consider:

- Reach out with the love of Jesus to an international student studying in your town or city.

- Search the Scriptures to find the answer to a coworker's difficult question.

- Drive all night to attend a funeral service of a person who demonstrated great faith in God.

- Open up enough to share with other guys some things you've learned from your mistakes and failures—even if you might be misunderstood or criticized.

Just think, as you accept the risks that accompany adventuring with God, you'll most certainly build a library of true stories—changed-life stories that will encourage you and encourage people you share them with.

Perhaps the most changed person of all will be you as you grow in relationship with God.

And God smiles.

———•———

Since I've already risked quite a bit in the Gunnison area and still have all my fingers and toes, I think I'll wait until it's warmer and the sun is up before bringing in more wood for the woodstove.

I wouldn't want to slip on the ice.

# 14

# Doubt, Discouragement, Danger

I used to think bad weather—pouring rain running down my neck, sleet blasting against my face, snow falling so heavily I can barely see 10 yards, dense fog darkening the woods—was the worst enemy I could face while hunting. An experience near a high mountain meadow revealed an even worse, insidiously harmful enemy.

Several friends and I set up camp near a reservoir in great elk country. We chose the site because of its proximity to steep, dense timber interrupted by long meadows in-between high ridges. After two days of hunting, I'd not even spotted an elk, but I'd seen fresh sign in the crusty snow so I knew they were in the area. After a quick breakfast of instant oatmeal by Coleman lantern light in the tent, I hiked up a winding trail. Several times I saw tracks of single elk— one going this way, one going that way. My steps quickened even though the trail was growing steeper and I was getting sweaty.

I couldn't wait to get to the high meadows and find a place downwind where I could see hundreds of yards in several directions. A strategy unfolded in my mind. *I'll ambush an elk that crosses a meadow either heading toward the top of this ridge or into one of those pockets of dark timber.* Carefully skirting the first meadow so I'd not be seen, I quietly walked around its perimeter to where it joined an even longer meadow. I found a great place, sat down on my waterproof pad behind a large pine tree, and waited expectantly, daydreaming about showing up at home with a huge elk. I was also shivering and wondering how long it would take the sun to get over the ridge I'd just crossed and shine down on me. The last hour before sunrise always seems to be the coldest part of the night.

As the sun finally rose, I waited impatiently for its rays to reach me. I opened my jacket and soaked up the welcomed heat. *What a great day!* I thought, looking down at my .30-06 cradled across my lap. *This Leupold scope is amazing. Maybe today I'll get to put its cross-hairs on an elk. I hope all of my preparation will pay off.*

I knew I'd chosen a good spot when a deer popped out across the meadow from me shortly after legal shooting light. It walked within 75 yards of me. I wished deer would do that when I was hunting them, but they always seem to know which license I have in my pack.

Hours passed; no elk appeared. I finally decided to find a new spot. Picking my way around deadfall, I started up an icy, rocky trail. Noticing that my left boot was untied, I leaned my rifle against a tree and knelt down to tie it.

Then it happened.

The barrel of my rifle slid off the tree trunk, and the scope hit a large rock—hard!

*Oh no!* I thought. *Is it okay?* Enthusiasm drained out of me like dirty oil from an oil pan. I quickly checked for obvious structural damage and didn't find any. *Here I am in a great place, my group is right where I want it to be, and now my scope will be off.* Doubt mixed with anger flooded my mind. *I could find the best spot right now, see an elk not far away, and miss my shot…just because I stupidly put my rifle on an icy spot on the trail.*

The rest of that day while I continued to hunt, scope-related doubt blasted into my thoughts again and again. So did self-criticism. *Why'd I do such a stupid thing?* The noise grew so loud in my head that I started getting bummed out. *Even if I get a shot right now I'll probably blow it because I'm too tense to shoot well. What's the use of hunting?*

I knew what I had to do in order to silence the doubt and discouragement. And I hated it. So many times I've gotten angry at other hunters who have done the same thing. I got some paper and a black marker out of my pack and improvised a target. I found a safe place to shoot, set up the target, paced off 100 yards, and fired several rounds into the target, no doubt scaring all nearby elk, deer, and porcupines. I also startled any hunters watching for animals during the golden, last-light-of-day moments. *Maybe they'll think I was shooting at an animal,* I hoped.

Amazingly, I hit the target both times. *The scope's just fine. Whew!* Since that time, I've become more sensitive to the paralysis of doubt. And to the different kinds of doubt I experience.

One kind sometimes surfaces when I try new things, like taking apart one of my chainsaws or mounting a winch on the bed of my truck. (When I was growing up, my failures were highlighted and praise was seldom given.)

Another kind of doubt relates to local and world issues. I wonder if our leaders will figure out how to resolve fiscal debt challenges and hold inflation in check.

The most dangerous kinds of doubt I experience, though, relate to my relationship with God:

- I can doubt God's promises in the Bible and lapse into inventing my own how-to principles for life. That usually includes depending on myself and trying to control situations and people to create the positive outcome I want.

- I can doubt God's forgiveness by allowing sins to fester inside my heart and mind instead of confessing them and releasing them to God.

- I can doubt God's willingness to answer prayer and not pray, at least about things I deem too difficult or too small for him to care about.

- I can doubt God's ongoing provision, especially when my checking account drops precipitously so I start worrying.

- I can doubt God's love for me and focus on hiding my weaknesses and predicating my identity on people's approval, adventures I've had, and things I possess rather than my identity as a disciple of Jesus.

- I can doubt God's blueprint for me by finding fault with the core of who I am.

- I can doubt God's willingness and ability to stand with me during difficult times by trying to become self-reliant and self-protective.

- I can doubt the value of God's church—the fellowship of followers of Jesus Christ—because of the ways I've been hurt by people in the church.

Why are such doubts so dangerous? When I doubt God, the foundation of my life crumbles. I revert to trying to deal with life on my own, in my own strength. I try to fix other people when I'm the real problem. I hide my insecurities and fears through more activity and anger. I'm tempted much more to think wrong thoughts and do things God wouldn't be happy about. In short, I lose equilibrium.

Fortunately God understands and lovingly draws me back to him. Yes, sometimes he does that using difficult circumstances. When my scope hit the rock and doubt flooded my mind for hours, that situation served as a simple-but-profound catalyst. Eventually I delved more deeply into my doubts and where they came from. Then I shared some of these "secret doubts" with godly men.

You know what I discovered? Other guys also experience doubt from time to time. Doubt about their self-worth. Doubt about God's character. Doubt about their parenting skills. Doubt about their marriages. Doubt about their future. They struggle with the same doubts I do!

I'm not as unique as I thought I was.

I don't have to be alone.

You know who else I'm discovering things about?

The God who sent his Son to die on a cross for my sins.

The Jesus who came back to life and offers not only eternal life but his Spirit within me wherever I am.

The God who labels himself "the Shepherd" and loves each of his sheep—even me—and demonstrates his love in all kinds of ways.

I'm realizing more about the God who loves me even after I fail, who desires to be in relationship with me even when I push him away, and who empowers me to be the courageous man he created me to be.

And this God—our God—will guide us through the irritations and doubts while respecting our uniqueness and our spiritual journeys. He'll give us joy and peace when we trust him.

When we realize a dangerous doubt about God has popped up,

why not think of it as a little tinkling bell on the end of a fishing pole or a pheasant being flushed from a cornfield? Use it as an encouragement to pay attention and take positive action based on biblical truth. The more we do this, the more we'll recognize such doubts more quickly, knowing that their roots lie in the evil one who hates God and desires to keep us from experiencing the life our loving God offers. The life we've always wanted.

Let's ask for God's help promptly…

- that he will replace lies we believe with his truths.

- that he will help us continue to walk as disciples of Jesus with steadfast hope, like we do on game trails.

- that he will remind us to be thankful for the faith in him that overcomes fear because such faith is built on his unchanging character.

- that he will help us understand that even when we can't "see" him or feel his presence, he is still our living God who knows everything about us and is unfolding his loving plans for us.

Are you wondering if I've ever put my rifle in a position where it could fall and damage the scope again? I plead the Fifth.

# 15

# Wounded

What started out to be a great afternoon of hunting went downhill fast. Two friends and I had hunted pronghorn for several days. We didn't start hunting until more than four weeks of the six-week season had passed, and the pronghorn we observed had wised up.

As we studied their movements from vantage points along the highway, we noticed that the herd spent late afternoons and nights in a little bowl. To their east, a large, treeless hill provided effective escape routes. To their north and south, open plains gave them excellent visibility and offered stalkers little cover.

After trying unsuccessfully to approach them from the west, we waited until they moved north—then evaluated where we might hide and get shots when they returned.

A small, mostly dried-up pond provided one option about 300 yards out, as did a corner fence of an electric substation and a nearby ravine. Plus, one of us could hide behind one of the huge electric poles running north and south.

About two o'clock, I walked out to the pond and worked my way to a spot where I could see the animals when they returned. I planned to ambush them if they ran south or west. My buddies remained near the substation.

An hour later, a few pronghorn returned to the bowl, but they were too far away for me to take a confident, ethical shot. I stood up and walked slowly east and north in a wide circle to see what they'd do when I got closer. If they ran northwest, my buddies might have a shot. If they ran southwest, I'd have a shot.

Several pronghorn ran toward my friends. A rifle cracked, and one pronghorn went down. The others panicked and angled south, still several hundred yards away from me. I had a shot at a running doe—and took it. A second later, she slowed to a trot. I've always desired immediate kills for humane reasons. But this time my bullet had hit a rear leg—a wound from which she probably wouldn't be able to recover.

Although I knew I might never catch up to her on foot, I started walking. She maintained a good pace but showed no inclination to move closer to the highway where she'd have to go under a fence to escape.

About 10 minutes later, she stopped several hundred yards away. Instead of taking my time, I hurried my shot…and missed. She took off, moving faster. I kept her in view for a while longer before losing her in some hills. *I don't want to stop now,* I thought. *I shot her. I'm going to find her.* I hate to see wounded animals in the field, and this time I'd crippled one. By now I was more than a mile from where I'd shot her, and the rolling hills limited visibility. Every time I'd come over a rise eager to see her…she'd be gone.

Finally I picked a route I hoped she took and hurried in that direction. Sure enough, there she was standing just below the top of a hill.

This time I didn't miss. As I walked up to her, I felt saddened and elated. Yes, I'd found her, but I'd caused her unnecessary pain.

I'm particularly sensitive to woundedness. As an elementary school-aged child attending a Christian school, I was bullied constantly. Tall, skinny, and uncoordinated, I was an easy target. I wasn't yet good in sports, so I also suffered the humiliation of almost always being picked last or next to last.

Later, I'd been excited to try out for the basketball team, but when I quickly lost the ball during a scrimmage with another school, the coach pulled me out immediately. I walked away ashamed.

I remember standing on the playground watching the other kids playing. I felt terribly alone and was starting to believe that I wasn't worth much to anyone, including God.

Then I made a decision that formed a cornerstone of my life.

*I'll show you,* I thought. *You think I'm nothing, but I'll show you I am something!* Anger replaced sadness and fueled my drive to be at least three steps ahead of anyone who might hurt me. I worked hard and practiced hard to prove myself by achievements. Success overshadowed my loneliness, fearful insecurities, and self-criticism. Self-focus ruled my life. I viewed myself as a fortified island. Strong on the outside and pretty tough on the inside so I'd feel no pain and never cry.

I know I'm not the only wounded hunter in this world. I'm sure I have lots of company.

I've learned that God's love, comfort, and forgiveness can heal the crippling wounds of the past.

Last night when I told my wife I planned to write about woundedness, she reminded me of a buck pronghorn we both saw one day while hunting. The buck led the herd, yet at a full run its gait was obviously different. We wondered why and soon realized a flap of dead skin was all that remained of its right front leg. The buck was running on three legs. Despite being wounded, he kept on trekkin'. And from the look of his harem, he was not just surviving, he was thriving! He was being a leader and protecting his females.

He wasn't off by himself hiding out.

He wasn't focused on his difficulties, though they obviously impacted his life.

No, he was actively living an adventurous life.

By God's grace, my raw wounds are healing. I'm gaining strength to finish living life well. Feeling like that three-legged buck sometimes, I'm striving to do what Paul wrote about: "I have fought the good fight, I have finished the race, I have kept the faith" (2 Timothy 4:7).

I'm running this earthly race for the long haul.

Will you join me?

I can't undertake this race alone. I need courageous, Christ-following guys who will stand with me and allow me to stand with them. Who will rejoice during times of victory and encourage during times of defeat.

This race is open to everybody everywhere.

The writer of the book of Hebrews describes the spiritual race God has for us, the focus we'll need, and the example Jesus—the ultimate long-distance runner—set for us:

> Let us throw off everything that hinders and the sin that so easily entangles. And let us run with perseverance the race marked out for us, fixing our eyes on Jesus, the pioneer and perfecter of faith. For the joy set before him he endured the cross, scorning its shame, and sat down at the right hand of the throne of God. Consider him who endured such opposition from sinners, so that you will not grow weary and lose heart (Hebrews 12:1-3).

Jesus' great love for each of us fueled his commitment to accomplish what he came to earth to do—acts that came with an extremely high cost.

He left heaven's glories to serve God on earth and redeem us.

He faced daunting challenges—scorn, abandonment, and physical pain.

He willingly chose to be wounded so we might be healed!

> [The LORD] was pierced for our transgressions,
>     he was crushed for our iniquities;
> the punishment that brought us peace was on him,
>     and by his wounds we are healed
>     (Isaiah 53:5; see also John 3:16).

Since Jesus' death and his resurrection three days later, the world has never been the same! And our race continues.

Jesus is with us each stride of the way.

# 16

# Brevity of Life

I'll never forget what I saw near the old gate of a pasture bordering national forest land. Anyone who loves animals wouldn't forget it either. Tracks in the snow recorded part of the story. A barbed-wire fence and the physical remains left in it recorded the rest.

No doubt the elk calf anticipated an early breakfast in my friend's hayfield. A few romps with other calves. The comforting presence of its mother. Fresh water. But the exuberant calf caught its leg inside two strands of wire while jumping the fence. As the calf's momentum drove it to the ground, the wire twisted. The animal's struggling tightened the wire.

No one knows how long this ordeal lasted. Maybe hours. Maybe a day.

When did the coyotes show up? They'd obviously eaten their fill, leaving a few bones, a leg, and pieces of picked-clean hide.

Why did this scene impact me deeply? I've seen dead animals in the field for years—sometimes from hunting parties, sometimes from Mother Nature's predators, sometimes from bone-chilling cold, five-foot snowdrifts, and gale-force winds. Perhaps it was because I could picture how quickly things changed for that calf.

My mind immediately went back to a time when my father-in-law nearly encountered death on a mountainside.

⋄

That day started out like so many other hunting days—oatmeal, a discussion about where we'd hunt and a final look at a topographic map, determining a rendezvous time and place in case we got separated, gathering our gear, and setting out.

The three of us—Walt, Roy, and I—decided to hunt an area of dense timber between two large meadows. We figured the elk would use trails hidden among the trees to avoid crossing the open space. As we headed up the steep slope, we spread out.

It was tough going—sections of thick scrub oak, slippery downed logs, icy rocks, deep ravines...As we stalked about 100 yards apart, clouds moved in from the north. They were dark and threatening, quite likely bringing additional snow to the 12 inches that had already fallen. The temperature was dropping too.

Having seen no elk, Walt and I took a break about 40 yards below the ridge. We paused to drink water, eat granola bars, and refine our strategy for the rest of the day. He'd scheduled the closing on his new home for later that week and didn't want to miss it.

Two hunters passed us along the top of the ridge, their canteens clanking loudly. Walt turned on his small weather radio to check on snowfall estimates. Just as the weatherman began speaking, Walt quietly exclaimed, "Bull elk!" and switched off the radio.

I turned my head and saw the largest bull elk I'd ever seen in the wild posing like a calendar photo less than 100 yards away. I raised my rifle; Walt did the same. We shot at nearly the same time.

Immediately the elk ran downhill to our left.

We hurried to where the elk had stood and tried to spot him. Elk, like other animals, can cover a lot of ground with bullets or arrows in them. We didn't want to lose him. If he was wounded and lying down with his head up, we'd watch him until he died before approaching. We spotted him on his haunches and watched as he fell over. We approached him carefully. When I touched his eyeball with the end of a stick, there was no response.

I opened my pack and got out my gear. We tied each hind leg to thick sagebrush branches with parachute cord and started the gutting process. It took longer than usual because of the elk's size and the position of his body. Moving him around was like trying to move a 16-hands-high horse.

As we were finishing, Roy approached, a huge smile on his face. "I heard your shots," he said. "I figured you had something down. This is a great elk!"

"It sure is," I replied. My shot had broken the front shoulder; Walt's shot had passed through the heart.

Snow began falling heavily; the wind became gusty. We assessed our needs and realized we'd have to pack out the meat, hide, and head. Our packs were at camp, more than a mile down steep terrain.

"I'll go get the pack frames," Roy volunteered, "while you guys get it skinned and boned out."

We agreed, and off he went.

As Walt and I worked, our fingers became numb from the cold. We boned out the meat and placed it in cotton pillowcases from my daypack to keep it clean. We worked as fast as we could—so fast that I hoped we wouldn't nick ourselves with our knives or pieces of sharp bone.

I wrapped my scarf around my neck and mouth, but the heat of my breath fogged up my glasses so I couldn't see. Off went the scarf, and the lenses gradually cleared. An hour or so later, the snowstorm moved in, creating nearly whiteout conditions. Walt and I decided to build a small fire to make it easier for Roy to spot us. I scrambled around to find dead limbs of pine trees, and dug dry pieces of wood out of deadfall logs. Somehow we managed to start and keep that little fire going.

After a while Walt said, "Shouldn't Roy be back by now?"

"I was wondering the same thing," I answered.

Half an hour later, Roy reached us. His words were a little slurred; his wool pants were icy. "I fell into the creek while crossing a narrow spot on the trail," he said. "Thanks for building the fire. I might have missed you up here otherwise."

Realizing he was exhausted and experiencing early stages of hypothermia, we added more wood to the fire and stayed there for nearly half an hour so he could warm up. While we waited, Walt and I tied the meat onto the pack frames.

Our descent was literally a *trip* at times. Walt and I each carried nearly 80 pounds of meat, and the deadfall and groundcover was slicker and icier than we remembered. Roy stayed with us, and as soon as we reached the tent he collapsed inside. It was the first and only time I've had to take off his boots and tuck him into a sleeping bag.

*Wow!* I thought. *What if we hadn't built that fire? What if he hadn't been wearing these wool pants when he landed in the creek? What if we hadn't stuck to our plan and were heading down as he climbed up and we missed each other?*

Roy might have died if the various factors hadn't come together well. And all three of us knew it. Even today, more than 30 years later, we recall that day as if it happened yesterday.

Exciting adventures—good or bad—are like that.

---

And as I stood there and stared at the remains of the elk calf in the barbed-wire fence, I considered how easy it is to ignore the ever-present reality of physical death. People spend billions of dollars trying to fend off the inevitable consequences of growing older—wrinkles, diminishing eyesight, brittle bones, gray hair, concentration decline (inability to do 15 tasks simultaneously, such as chew granola, watch the horizon, listen for a leaf being crunched, figure out how big the approaching deer really is, shiver from the cold, be grateful for a plastic pee bottle). Fitness center managers promise to guide us in postponing the inevitable muscle loss, and gyms and spas often have mirrors so we can compare ourselves to others.

Yet the truth of life and death surfaces again and again.

Wherever we live.

Whatever we hunt.

Whoever we know.

However we prepare.

No matter how well we plan our time.

No matter how much or how little sleep we get.

As soon as we are born, we are terminal. (I said this once in the health club I use, and a guy in his early thirties replied, "That's profound. I never thought of that before.")

There are no exceptions to this aspect of life.

Every living thing dies.

There are no opportunities to hit a "redo" or "refresh" button and start life over again. (Think of all the hunting lore we'd already know! Oh well…)

We don't know when death will come, and we seldom know what the cause of our deaths will be. We may experience a tragic accident, like that calf elk, die at age 90, or contract a disease. Whatever the timetable, like the flowers and grasses we each experience an all-too-brief life. Then we breathe our last breaths.

Death became more real to many Americans when terrorists used airplanes to bring down the Twin Towers of the World Trade Center in New York City on September 11, 2001.

Death hit closer to home for me shortly after that. My mother's friends came and sat with her as she lay dying from cancer. They talked to her, sang to her, and read Bible verses to her. She couldn't speak, yet we knew she heard everything.

I stood near my mother's side as cancer finally took her life. Later I watched strangers move her frail body out the door. The psalmist and other biblical writers studied nature and often used common, everyday images to emphasize their points. David wrote, "The life of mortals is like grass, they flourish like a flower of the field; the wind blows over it and it is gone, and its place remembers it no more" (Psalm 103:15-16).

These reflections about mortality bring to mind a recent, sobering event that happened near my home in Colorado. While driving into town, I saw a mangled SUV and badly damaged truck on the side of the road. I pulled over and walked back to see if I could offer assistance. Although no law enforcement personnel had arrived, four paramedics were down in a ditch near a culvert trying to resuscitate a 30-something woman.

From the looks of the vehicles, the woman didn't notice a stop sign and, halfway through the intersection, the pickup had broadsided her car. The woman died the next day. A cross and fake flowers still mark that spot.

I've been thinking quite a bit about life and death.

About making my life count.

About what God desires to accomplish in me by shaping me into a more godly man, husband, father, and friend. I've got a long way to go in getting there, but I know I'm on the right path.

When I die, I don't think it'll really matter what hunting gear I leave behind. In fact, none of my possessions—not even my blackpowder rifles—will mean much. No matter who gets them and how well they are cared for, all that stuff will fade away, rust away, maybe even be stolen. Some of it just burned up when the large Black Forest Fire (Colorado Springs, 2013) went through our property. My only *legacy* will be people—those I have loved and cherished. Those whom God placed under my care. Those with whom I've discussed issues more important than hunting seasons and stories.

Did I love my wife and daughter and tenderly care for them?

Did I demonstrate compassion toward hurting people?

Did I use the time I had well?

I like what the psalmist David wrote:

> Show me, LORD, my life's end
>> and the number of my days;
>> let me know how fleeting my life is.
> You have made my days a mere handbreadth;
>> the span of my years is as nothing before you.
> Everyone is but a breath,
>> even those who seem secure (Psalm 39:4-5).

I also like this line from "a prayer of Moses":

> Teach us to number our days,
>> that we may gain a heart of wisdom
>> (Psalm 90:12).

The other day I received a precious text from my daughter: "You are a fantastic father, and I am blessed with you!" I immediately thought, *Me? Really?* A while later I uttered this prayer: "Thanks, God, for giving me today…and for standing with me as I keep trying to be a better husband, father, and friend."

# 17

# Forgiveness

When you hear the word "forgiveness," you probably don't immediately think of a hunting trip.

I do.

For several days, my longtime friends Walt and Roy had been hunting pronghorn with me on a ranch north of Laramie, Wyoming. We first heard about the ranch through my wife's cousin, and after I made a few phone calls we received permission to hunt six pronghorn there—two apiece—if we drew tags. So we applied, and months later the tags arrived! I couldn't wait to get out and hunt, and my anticipation increased even more when the rancher told me that bordering ranches west and north didn't allow hunting and, therefore, large herds of pronghorn sometimes grazed on his land.

The history of the ranch reads like a movie script. The small ranch house ended up where it is—in a low spot on the prairie—because the wagon carrying building supplies broke down right there in the late 1800s. An old Model T in very good condition is parked in a dusty corner inside the barn. And the collection of "inventory" (another word for junk) in the field includes ancient tractor parts and many pieces of equipment I couldn't identify.

Walt, Roy, and I felt privileged to truly take a step back into history and do what most Native American tribes, as well as many settlers, had done before us—hunt pronghorn for meat. As late as the 1870s, a train passenger described a 70-mile-long herd of pronghorn grazing on the plains.

Because the ranch at one time raised sheep, huge pastures had perimeters of expensive "sheep fence"—multiple strands of barbed wire pulled tight to make it hard for sheep to escape and coyotes to get in. That fencing gave hunters like us an edge because pronghorn aren't jumpers so they typically crawl *under* fencing. And they can't crawl under sheep fence unless a ditch going under it has deepened or a wire breaks. We spent the first two days hunting in areas without such fences.

Walt and I each shot our two pronghorn, and Roy shot one. During our last full day of the hunt, we chose an area northeast of the ranch house where a herd of pronghorn were grazing at one end of the pasture. There were several nearby outbuildings in various stages of disrepair and not much else. Early that morning, we drove to within half a mile of the herd and worked up a strategy. Conveniently, the pronghorn didn't move much, clearly not worried about us.

Our strategy was simple. We'd approach from the north. I'd work my way in a large arc west, where the pronghorn could see me. I'd be the "blocker," whose presence would deter them from moving west. Walt would go a bit northeast and maintain a visible presence there. Roy would set up in the middle near an old building so he could shoot when the pronghorn moved closer. We knew they'd probably not go south and cross the main highway. Also we didn't see any openings in the sheep fence.

I took my time, moving slowly and steadily in a large circle, far enough away from the pronghorn not to spook them yet close enough for them to see me. When I got to my designated spot, I sat down in the dirt near an old fence post and waited.

Ten minutes went by, and the pronghorn didn't move.

Twenty minutes went by…

Half an hour went by…

Getting restless, I came up with a new strategy. *I'll stand up and walk toward the animals while staying south near the sheep fence. That way the animals will be forced to move toward Roy, and he can get his shot. They won't come toward me or Walt, and we won't have to wait for hours for them to move.*

Deep inside, I knew what I was doing was wrong. It's always important for hunters to stick with agreed-upon strategies and not change things up for convenience when isolated from the others. *But this time,* I rationalized, *things will work out well.*

Off I went, heading straight south toward the fence. Keeping it to my right, I walked east toward the pronghorn. Immediately several does stood up, and the lead buck stared at me intently. A few more does, now on alert, milled around restlessly, concerned about my presence yet unsure what to do or where to go. Clearly they didn't want to remain in the corner, and no doubt they could see Walt.

*It's going to work,* I thought. *They'll go right by Roy.*

Then everything changed.

The lead buck started trotting, motivating the entire herd to run *toward me* at 45 or so miles per hour.

I picked up my pace, walking quickly toward the middle and straight toward the buck, determined to get them to turn north toward Roy.

They kept coming!

No more than 15 seconds later, the entire herd thundered past me about 30 yards away, determined to run west at all costs. In disbelief, I watched them get smaller and smaller as they ran away. Then all of them scrambled under the sheep fence using a small ravine I hadn't noticed and headed toward the horizon.

*I sure blew it this time!* I thought. *Not only did I mess up the strategy, I likely kept Roy from getting his second pronghorn. We have to leave soon, and that herd is long gone. And they've crossed onto the neighboring ranch that doesn't allow hunting.* Shuffling along, not eager to meet up with Roy and Walt, I realized my impatience combined with pride had spoiled everything.

"Why'd you do that?" Walt asked in a tone tinged with surprise and anger when we all met near our vehicle. "We had a good strategy working. Those pronghorn would have moved where we wanted them within an hour or two."

Roy just looked at me, disappointment in his eyes.

I felt ashamed. "I wanted to get them moving past you right away," I said weakly, waiting for one of them to criticize me and tell me how stupid I'd been.

Both of them nodded.

I was very tempted to defend my actions so I wouldn't seem like an idiot hunter, but I knew what I had to do.

A short time later, I did it.

I apologized to Roy.

You know what? He didn't go on a tirade telling me what a foolish thing I'd done. He knew I knew that already. Nor did he say something like, "You know, we've hunted together all this time and still

you decided to do *that*?" I certainly deserved that kind of response…
or possibly one much worse.

Roy simply accepted my apology, forgave me, and went about the
usual business of hunting.

I was really surprised. No, not because I'd expected Roy to act any
different, but because I grew up being blamed, shamed, and criticized for mistakes I made or for not measuring up to impossible
standards. I was already prepared to defend myself from my buddies, but no defense was necessary. Roy simply forgave me. Nothing much else was said later about what I'd done either. All three of
us knew I'd never make the mistake of changing the strategy on my
own again.

I learned a great deal about forgiveness that day.

Forgiveness doesn't have strings attached, such as damaging
criticism.

Forgiveness isn't, "I forgive you, but…"

Forgiveness is freely offered.

Forgiveness heals and restores.

Forgiveness lifted my spirit, and I sure felt better afterward.

Certainly most of us make decisions or mistakes that in some
way inconvenience other hunters or even ruin a day's hunting experience. It may be driving a four-wheeler up an old logging road
where a hunter has been sitting since before dawn. It may be getting stuck at a spot on a muddy road where no one can drive past.
It may be firing up a generator too early in the morning or taking a
leak along a trail only to discover a hunter just around the bend who
didn't want human scent by "his" trail.

The ultimate act of forgiveness, one I can't fully comprehend,
took place more than 2000 years ago. Jesus, who committed no sin
even when in human form, took all our sins on himself by hanging
on a cross in agony until his death. Why? To pay for our sins so we can
be in true relationship with our holy God and receive forgiveness for
our sins and eternal life. Jesus paid the ultimate price that we owed.

Consider these words about God's forgiveness: "If we confess our sins, [God] is faithful and just and will forgive us our sins and purify us from all unrighteousness" (1 John 1:9). What's "unrighteousness"? First John 3:7 defines a righteous person simply as "the one who does what is right." So "unrighteousness" basically means actions and thoughts that aren't in line with biblical teaching.

Isn't that amazing? No matter what wrongdoing you and I have done, God will forgive us and establish us in a personal relationship with him if we ask Him. And he will continue to forgive us when we mess up. And that's not all! God encourages us to do much more than just ask him for forgiveness. Paul, with the inspiration of the Holy Spirit, wrote these words to the Colossian followers of Jesus: "Bear with each other and forgive one another if any of you have grievances against someone. *Forgive as the Lord forgave you.* And over all these virtues put on love, which binds them all together in perfect unity" (Colossians 3:13-14).

What a challenge! We are to forgive as the Lord forgives us.

No strings attached.

No excuses because of what another person did first.

No verbal forgiveness that isn't really from our hearts.

No forgiveness given for only certain categories of sins.

No forgiveness extended for only a specific number of sins.

No forgiveness given just to show other people we're pretty good folks.

Jesus forgives all our sins when we turn to him as our Lord and Savior. And if you're anything like me, you've committed more than your share of secret sins as well as obvious sins.

May each of us remember God's amazing depth of forgiveness and, in his power, choose to forgive others.

Roy did.

That means more to me than I can express.

# 18

# Following Wise Counsel

When we entered the cabin we'd rented for deer season, the three of us knew several things immediately:

- It was a good thing we brought water—the cabin's water had been turned off for the winter.

- The closest toilet wasn't down the hall because there was no hall. The privy was a ways out the front door.

- We'd barely have room to turn over in our bunks.

- It was a good thing we'd brought a heater and propane stove. We knew we wouldn't want to coax the antique woodstove into use for an hour or more after hunting all day.

- The prize feature of the cabin that outweighed everything else was the fact that the property bordered public hunting land. We could just drive through a few gates and start hunting where few other hunters would be.

Life couldn't be better. After all, grown men need a bit more adventure in life, right? And if we got tired of too many adventures, what were we doing hunting anyway? I could hardly wait to head out the door the next morning to start hunting. The habitat was ideal—a creek running through the area, hayfields all around, and a mixture of high promontories and huge open areas for the deer.

After the usual friendly banter over a huge one-pot dinner, we put our plastic silverware in a bag to take home to the dishwasher and prepared our gear for the next day. We turned in for the night excited about the next day's opportunities.

Early in the morning, we ate a quick breakfast (we seldom take time for a big breakfast unless it's snowing really hard, raining really hard, or mice have kept us up all night by their scrambling around) and hopped into the four-wheel-drive to head out. After traversing a particularly soggy part of a hayfield, we went through a gate and started hunting immediately. Perhaps 10 minutes later, we came upon a little cabin down a hill to our right. Right behind the hill stood a huge pile of boulders—a spot I couldn't wait to climb to do some scouting.

My friends dropped me off and drove a distance away. It took me a little while to get over the fence next to the road, and then I headed to the left of the cabin and worked my way up the hill. My

.243 hanging from its sling over my shoulder, I reached the top of the boulders in a few minutes.

Suddenly I saw deer—about 12 of them! I couldn't believe it. I eased my way behind a rock and readied my Springfield A303 .30-06. They were only about 100 yards away, so I didn't bother to use my binoculars. I just steadied my gun, put the crosshairs on a large one, and fired once.

The herd stampeded away.

Expecting to see a deer lying on the ground, I stood up.

No deer.

No sounds of an animal's kicking feet or labored breathing.

Just my disappointed thoughts clamoring for attention.

I walked slowly over to where the deer had been standing, searching for sign. When I reached the spot where "my deer" had stood, there wasn't even a drop of blood. No clump of hair either. Working out from my target area, I tried to figure out systematically where that deer went. I was certain I'd hit it.

As I walked around up there, I must have looked pretty comical to my friends watching from below. Back and forth I walked, head down as I searched.

No blood.

No deer.

Suddenly I noticed that my friends had driven closer to me, and both of them were trying to signal me. I got my binoculars out and glassed them, trying to interpret their hand motions.

*They want me to come toward them,* I realized. So I did. After going around another huge boulder, I looked at them again. *Now they want me to go down.* My rifle at the ready in case my deer was wounded and moving, I started down. Still no blood trail or deer visible. *This makes no sense; why are they directing me down here?* I wondered.

After going around several more boulders and nearly reaching flat ground, I finally saw my deer tucked in-between some rocks. I was really happy! I was also wondering how I might improve my tracking ability. Fortunately my observing friends had seen everything. In fact, they told me later they saw the deer before I did and watched as I took the shot. They saw the deer flinch and then run with the others toward the base of the hill. They also watched it stagger and drop.

They knew the outcome long before I figured it out. Based on my trust in them, I'd responded to their signals even though they made no sense to me. If I hadn't noticed my friends or had ignored what they were communicating through their hand signals because I thought I knew better, I might have spent quite a while hunting for my deer.

Have you ever pondered Proverbs 12:15? "The wise listen to advice." It's so easy to get caught up in our individuality and personal achievements in trying to be "successful" on our own. For a long time I did this. Now, partly due to hunting with wise friends, I've come to recognize the higher value of living in and with a community of special people. I participate in a large men's group at church who genuinely care about me and have helped my family and me in various ways.

I need people who will speak truth into my life even though I may not like to hear what they say sometimes.

I need people who care enough to observe what I'm doing and to provide guidance when I'm a bit lost or confused.

Of course, quite a bit of responsibility also falls on me. I need to keep myself open to feedback from godly people. To make sure their advice is biblical and then follow their directions even when I'm not sure of the outcome. To willingly let go of my own agendas in order to fall in line with God's ongoing plans for my life.

Because of people like my hunting partners—people who choose to be in companionship with me—I'm able to locate animals I've shot, and I'm more confident as I face life's challenges. With wise people at my side, I don't feel alone on this spinning planet. I know that no matter what, God has given me his wisdom and the advice of close family and friends to tap into.

Because of that, I am able to take the path less traveled…God's path…no matter what life dishes out.

And that makes all the difference.

# Perseverance

I badly needed a peaceful hunting trip. Instead I got several days of intense challenges. It all started when a former neighbor (I'll call him Duane) asked, "How'd you like to hunt elk east of Gunnison, Colorado, with a friend and me in October? And you can bring your pop-up trailer, right?"

"Sure!" I answered, my happiness meter pegging off the chart. *With a guy like this leading our hunting party, we'll have a great hunt!* I thought. Duane had set up drop camps before and brought home meat from hunting quite often. He even gave Amanda and me more than 100 pounds of boneless elk meat when his wife grew tired of eating game. And I knew that where he was talking about hunting had a resident elk herd plus other elk migrated through the area when heavy snows hit the high country.

Two weeks before our elk season started, I sorted gear, sighted in my .30-06 (two inches high at 100 yards using 180-grain bullets), and bought my over-the-counter "four points or better" bull elk license. In addition to the usual items, I added a Coleman stove, kerosene heater, and small tent "just in case."

Finally departure day arrived. My excitement bubbled up like the geysers I'd seen at Yellowstone as I hooked up the pop-up trailer to my Scout Traveler and followed Duane's diesel Blazer down the highway. Four hours later, we reached a narrow, partially frozen road heading into the national forest. After our vehicles churned mud for about a mile and a half, Duane stopped, got out of his vehicle, and approached my Scout. I quickly rolled down the window.

"Now we go up there," he stated, pointing to the left.

*Up there?* I thought and gulped. I gazed at the hairpin, rock-and-boulder-strewn, icy road. It looked more like an oversized path with tire ruts. Visualize the inside slope of a banana when one end is on the table and the other mostly points toward the ceiling. Now add large rocks, mud, a heavy trailer, and a tired Scout engine that emits smoke.

My mental calculator exclaimed, "No way!"

I should have paid attention to it and stated my misgivings.

Instead, I nodded in agreement and followed Duane after he got into his vehicle and headed up the hill. I listened to awful noises as the Scout dragged the pop-up across rocks for the next 10 minutes. I felt like how a warm-water tortoise might feel dragging another tortoise up an icy ski hill.

At the crest of a ridge, I figured we'd camp near the small meadows nearby. Duane had different ideas. Up we went for another mile. The increasing snow level dramatically reminded me of an Alaskan postcard with a winter scene. My Scout was sliding now, especially when we got on another wide trail near a deep, boulder-strewn ravine. Steering uphill, I made it to the top and breathed a sigh of relief.

Then it started to snow. Huge flakes! After what seemed like hours but was probably 45 minutes, Duane parked on a high plateau. We set up camp with 14 inches of wet snow crunching under our boots. Sadly, I hardly noticed the breath-taking mountains, open valley, and dense forest just below timberline. Even with my wool cap, my ears got cold.

As I cranked up my pop-up, the front half suddenly dropped

about four feet. It looked like a crushed box arriving via the postal service on Christmas Eve. The top wouldn't move. I discovered that a rock had struck a primary cable, and the trailer had called it quits. Permanently.

I felt like a rabbit trapped inside a vegetable garden fence with a dog. There was no escape. Revealing the obvious, I told Duane and his friend, who by this time were staring at the pop-up, "I can't fix this." Our designated place to eat, sleep, store gear, and get warm mockingly swayed in the increasing wind. I discovered soon enough that the reason Duane had invited me on the hunt had just collapsed.

Trying to avoid Duane's dirty looks, I erected my small tent on the snow and crawled into my sleeping bag after grabbing a few bites of snack food. *I hope tomorrow will be better*, I thought.

I've forgotten Duane's comments as he pitched his own back-up tent, and that's probably a good thing.

Sometimes snow drifts down in little flakes, like pieces of down from a punctured pillow. Not this time. Shivering, I had to come out of the tent and erect a tarp over it. I had to get up and knock snow off it several times during the night to avoid being buried alive in a flattened tent. By morning the snow was still coming down—about three inches every hour—and the weight was tearing out the tarp's grommets.

*It's decision time*, I realized. *Stay or leave now even though it is opening morning of elk season. Perhaps a bull elk 400 yards away is pawing through all this snow to reach grass or is leading his herd south and will pass close by. And I don't quit when times get hard, right?* I decided to take the smart route and get that pop-up out of there immediately. It was that or likely visit what was left of it in the spring after the snow had melted. With the tone of a stern boss, I asked, "Which of you will help me get this back to the highway?"

"No way I'm missing opening morning!" Duane exclaimed.

His friend agreed to go with me—probably from guilt.

My tires kept spinning despite their chains, and we nearly slid off the road numerous times. When we got down, we left the trailer parked at a nearby ranch. Returning to camp was *déjà vu*. Just when things seemed better, the Scout slid backward on a steep hill and could go no higher. We ran out cable from the old Warn winch mounted on the front of my Scout and hooked it to a nearby aspen tree. We placed an old sleeping bag across the cable in case it snapped back. The cable tightened. The Scout moved about eight feet, and then the shallow-rooted tree tumbled across the road in front of us. We cut the tree into seven-foot sections with a bow saw, dragged them to the side, and hooked the cable to a larger aspen. Yep, it also fell across the road. Only one more huge aspen tree promised deliverance. If it fell, the Scout would have a new hood design…or worse. Fortunately, this tree only quivered.

Finally arriving back at the campsite, we parked, I got my gear, and we hunted along a high ridge overlooking the valley for several hours. Sometimes snow reached my thighs, and often I felt like I was pushing rather than walking. Fading elk tracks in the snow within the dark timber, an area dense with trees and thick underbrush, pointed south like a neon sign announcing ten-cent burgers every Wednesday for families with five or more children under age ten.

Returning to camp, I announced, "I'm leaving!" I began taking down my tent.

"Not until you use your extra propane heater to heat up my Blazer's oil pan so it'll start," Duane replied.

*Wait a minute!* I thought. *You drove up here knowing your diesel engine wouldn't start if it got cold and not knowing whether I'd even bring an extra heater?* I don't remember if I kicked a tire in frustration, or bit my lip, or muttered quietly. Probably another good thing to have forgotten.

Two hours later the Blazer started, and I left immediately. On my way down, I slid by an overturned four-wheel-drive lodged among boulders in that treacherous ravine. I picked up the pop-up, which

I left an hour later in a small town, and headed to Pagosa Springs where a ranch owner agreed to let me sleep in an unused cabin. (I discovered why it was unused later.)

As late-afternoon shadows grew, I slogged up a steep ridge and sat where I could observe several game trails. Within 20 minutes, I heard loud noises. *Wow, is that hunter noisy,* I thought. Moments later eight elk stampeded right at me for reasons I'll never know. Startled, I finished counting four points on the largest bull as he leaped past me less than 10 feet away. I shot him through the neck seconds later when he stuck his head up about 50 feet below me in scrub oaks. I figured he was trying to locate his cows.

After gutting the elk—no easy feat on that slope—I marked the spot in my usual way (you know how much coyotes hate human urine) and headed back to the ranch. A ranch hand agreed to bring horses up to get my elk the next morning, and I eagerly headed to the unheated cabin. It had more holes in the half-chinked walls than a pegboard. No wonder the ranch owner was pleased to get $20 for my air-conditioned lodging. It was the first time I'd slept inside a building when, if I looked more closely, I might have learned about several constellations through the rafters at the southern end. Needless to say, I never bothered to get a fire going in the Civil War-era woodstove.

The next morning, stiff and somewhat groggy, I hauled batches of deboned elk meat to the top of the ridge while awaiting the guy with the packhorses. He finally arrived, his face pea-green from partying with a nearby lady rancher most of the night. As he lay on the ground watching me, he kept repeating, "Load those horses evenly. Can't be more than a pound or two off!"

Balance, I realized, is key when packing a load on a horse. Otherwise, as the horse moves down the trail, the load rocking back and forth will shift. But I didn't have a portable scale up there, and most of the meat was in large sections that made even weight distribution difficult. Fortunately, due to beginner's luck I think, the loads on the horses didn't settle or shift on the way down.

As I drove home very early the following morning, I felt proud…
and exhausted. I'd completed a successful hunt despite far too many
obstacles. I'd rediscovered the value of woolen long johns, a little
heater, and an extra tent. Even today my fingertips remind me of
those special days by turning a bit white whenever I forget to wear
gloves during cold weather.

As I write these words sitting in my warm, comfortable home
office, I think of other difficulties I've faced. A beloved cousin
dying suddenly. The miscarriage of Amanda's and my first child.
Job stresses. Discs in my back damaged. Struggles to find spiritual
faith before discovering the loving, grace-giving God of the Bible. A
friend facing the ravages of Parkinson's Disease.

Yet sometimes I still find myself expecting—even demanding—
that my walk with God and my life experiences on this earth will get
easier and less rigorous. Do you know what I'd really like?

- A perfect marriage—comfortable bliss year after year
  with no disagreements and no miscommunication.

- No more times when my prayers seem to bounce off the
  ceiling and God seems far away.

- No mean-spirited people in heavy traffic.

- No alluring temptations wearing skirts.

- No financial crises in government.

- No huge health insurance premium increases.

- No irritating neighbors singing karaoke at one o'clock in
  the morning during the summer when our house windows are open.

- No vindictive bosses or career path dead ends.

- No exhaustion from caregiving.

- No stopped-up toilets.

- No struggles to hear God's voice amid cultural noise.

- No friends losing children to disease.
- No physical pain demanding self-preoccupation.
- No fears of any kind.
- No more times of feeling hungry, angry, lonely, tired, or stressed.

I'm sure you could add many other things to my list. But life on earth isn't like that. And you know what? I think God smiles at my thoughts because he knows what's best for me amid this earthly life and delights in my desire to know him better and keep trusting him no matter how I feel. I also think God cries sometimes when I experience pain and sorrow, just as Jesus cried after his friend Lazarus died ( John 11:17-35).

God diligently offers his Spirit to live in me so I can persevere in his power and find encouragement in his presence, in his wisdom recorded in the Bible, and in fellowship with other followers of Jesus Christ.

God takes spiritual perseverance quite seriously. Check this out from James: "Consider it pure joy, my brothers and sisters, whenever you face trials of many kinds" ( James 1:2). This is a cosmic shift from the "it's all about me" teachings so prevalent in today's world. It's not a "follow God and get all that you desire" theology either. No, it's a serious, countercultural, "burst through the snowdrifts and get a fire going with wet wood without using fire starter" teaching.

James continues, "because you know that the testing of your faith produces perseverance" (1:3). Hmmm. Yes, some of my most crucial life lessons—and the source of many hunting stories—have been forged during quite-stressful, no-apparent-relief moments strung together to create extremely challenging minutes, hours, days, weeks, months, and years. Even though I know God is helping me grow, I can't help but talk to him:

*Hey, God, can't I take a shortcut and miss most of life's difficulties because I've already learned quite a bit?*

*What happens, God, if I decide not to let you form me into who you desire me to be? If I stop marching forward and try to find my own shade amid life's scorching heat? Is it really worthwhile to keep stepping out in faith and trusting you to unfold your unique plans for my life?*

Fortunately God, through James, isn't done speaking about perseverance. "Let perseverance finish its work so that you may be mature and complete, not lacking anything" (James 1:4). Ah, an objective unfolds for each of us. Hope calls out like a joyous bluebird near her garden nesting box.

After a few more verses, God's truth thunders forth again, focusing on the blessing in-between the surviving and thriving aspects of life. It's found in verse 12. Do you see it? "Blessed is the one who perseveres under trial because, having stood the test, that person will receive the crown of life that the Lord has promised to those who love him."

Did you get that? I mean *really* get that? This blessing is for you and me.

When we persevere in godly ways, God blesses us! When we persevere through difficulties, surveying our options and trying to understand what we may never understand on this earth, God reaches down. He gently places a loving hand on our shoulders and provides a renewed sense of himself and his promises in our struggling hearts and minds. He reorients our tendency to focus inward and guides us toward his eternal glory that all who have placed their faith in Jesus will experience.

Jesus knows all about perseverance. He stood his ground and used Scripture to battle Satan and his temptations. Jesus kept doing his Father's will even when his human family thought he was crazy and Jewish religious leaders persecuted him savagely. When only one of ten lepers he healed returned praising God and wanting to thank Jesus, the Lord kept healing people rather than sinking into cynicism.

As the day approached for him to be crucified and take the sins of all humankind on himself as the sacrificial Lamb of God, Jesus steadfastly walked to Jerusalem and reminded his disciples that they too would face suffering. Jesus didn't disappear into the desert.

The night before he was to be arrested, he went to the Garden of Gethsemane to pray. He earnestly asked his Father to remove the dreadful task ahead of him, and then submitted to his Father's will. When the mob came, Jesus surrendered peacefully. Later, on the cross with nails punched through his hands and feet, his scalp ripped open by a crown of thorns, Jesus prayed for those who had crucified him, took humankind's sins on himself, and died after

uttering words that pointed everyone to his heavenly Father. Jesus was buried in a tomb, but three days later conquered death by coming to life again. After visiting and teaching his disciples and others for 40 days, Jesus returned to heaven (Acts 1:3; Luke 24:50-51).

Perseverance eternally rewarded.

Eternal options for us provided.

Want to know a secret? The large head of that four-point bull elk I shot that hunting season is mounted in our home's entry hall. Its rack isn't large—certainly not the usual take-up-the-entire-wall trophy mount. Some might ask, "Why'd you pay hundreds of dollars to have that mounted?" But you won't.

You know it's all about remembering the value of perseverance.

# 20

# Warfare

Swirling storm clouds blew toward us as we drove up a steep hill. When we reached the top, binoculars in hand, we got out of the vehicle and studied the long valley and foothills to the north looking for pronghorn.

"I see a small herd," Walt said, "about 900 yards east."

Immediately I tried to locate it. This was our last attempt to get an additional animal. We had five pronghorn hanging, but Walt had tags for two more and I had a tag for one more. As light rain began to fall, I wondered if we could stay in this area. The clay-based dirt, when wet, makes traveling off paved roads nearly impossible. *If we don't get an animal soon,* I thought, *we'll have to go home with what we have and call it good.*

We got back into the vehicle, and I drove slowly on the road heading east. The pronghorn were watching us and milling around nervously.

"That buck and one doe are separating from the herd," Walt said enthusiastically. "Drive up and around this next hill. I know where these two will go."

I recalled our experiences in this area two days earlier. We'd stalked 10 or so animals. But, as is often the case, they seemed to just disappear—quite likely going into the deep ravines that provide shelter for deer, elk, coyotes, foxes, and other animals.

Just when we thought nothing exciting would happen that day, a lone buck had headed right toward us, as if he knew we only had doe tags! Faster and faster he ran. To my amazement, he then turned and hightailed it right between my father-in-law and me.

Did Roy hide behind a rock? No.

Was he ready with a camera? No.

He waited until that buck was within 40 yards, and then stood up and made the funniest noises I've ever heard. The buck kept coming, and Roy made even louder noises. "Aaaaaahh. Yahhhhhhhh. Aaaaaahh. Yahhhhhhhh." The buck suddenly turned and ran back onto the plain, a thin cloud of dust rising in the air behind him.

*Wow, he sure is beautiful!* I noted. *How well adapted he is for the conditions up here. I hope we can see him and those does again. If he'd been a doe, we'd have shot her.*

Coming back to the present, I got my rifle ready. As soon as the Jeep stopped, Walt and I got out and hurried toward the base of the hill.

Walt sat down and positioned himself for a shot.

I sat down about five yards to his left.

Perhaps the same buck from the other day was circling this hill again and bringing a doe with him…

I'm sure in *real time* those two pronghorn rounded that hill less than 15 seconds after we sat down. But to me it seemed like 4 or 5 seconds. I was so excited! Both pronghorn rocketed into view, angling away from us toward the left. Walt took a 100-yard shot, and the doe dropped immediately. Perplexed, the buck slowed down and stopped.

Often I've seen bucks respond like this.

"Great shot!" I exclaimed, knowing that Walt almost became a U.S. Army sniper during the Vietnam War. For him, this was normal shooting. During the time before hunting season, he stays on target by shooting coyotes.

Walt smiled and walked back to get the Jeep as I headed to the doe to begin the gutting process. This was a mighty fun way to end our hunt, for sure.

As I replay events of that hunting day in my mind, I ponder Walt's words: "I know where these two will go."

As you no doubt know, big-game animals use a variety of escape routes. They go up, down, sideways, and diagonally. In this case, the buck had learned to run up to and circle this particular hill. By using information he'd gleaned days earlier, Walt anticipated where both animals would go when they were spooked. The buck experienced the escape he'd hoped for, but only because we had doe tags. The doe with him didn't have a chance.

There are many parallel situations in life. At various times I've used escape routes that promised to provide relief from threats and stresses in my life. I worked way too hard to prove that I had self-worth. I've used alcohol to "take the edge off" stress. I've tried to figure out "a system" and accumulate enough money to be financially secure. I've believed the excuses I came up with for not cherishing my wife enough. None of these worked well, and all of them created negative consequences.

Walt anticipated where that buck and doe would run based on knowledge. Through God's Word, the Bible, we are given the knowledge that Satan—an evil being—watches us so he can use our weaknesses to prey on us and try to get us to turn away from God. The apostle Paul wrote this to the church in Ephesus and to us:

> For our struggle is not against flesh and blood, but against the rulers, against the authorities, against the powers of this dark world and against the spiritual forces of evil in the heavenly realms. Therefore put on the full armor of God, so that when the day of evil comes, you may be able to stand your ground, and after you have done everything, to stand. Stand firm then, with the belt of truth buckled around your waist, with the breastplate

of righteousness in place, and with your feet fitted with the readiness that comes from the gospel of peace.

In addition to all this, take up the shield of faith, with which you can extinguish all the flaming arrows of the evil one. Take the helmet of salvation and the sword of the Spirit, which is the word of God.

And pray in the Spirit on all occasions with all kinds of prayers and requests. With this in mind, be alert and always keep on praying for all the Lord's people (Ephesians 6:12-18).

When I reflect on my life so far, various times when I have fallen short come to mind.

Times when I chose to become bitter because people treated me wrongly.

Times when anger bubbled up from my unresolved issues.

Times when I quit praying for a while because of false beliefs about God.

Times when it was easier to do wrong things than to stand firm and do right things with God's help and power.

To put it bluntly, Satan often took me out of the game by tearing me down, causing me to be a person who wasn't uplifting or fun to be around. He reduced my potential for God and life.

Many people today laugh at the thought that evil spiritual beings exist and desire to attack us. But those beings are real. They watch us to discover our strengths and corresponding weaknesses so they can bring us down. Satan and his evil horde hit us hard and often.

Exploiting our weaknesses.

Ambushing us so we turn away from the abundant life God promises his followers.

Sidetracking us into wrongdoing that damages our relationships with God, our relationships with people, and even the deepest parts of our hearts and minds.

Paul cautions, "Do not give the devil a foothold" (Ephesians 4:27). This image reminds me of times when I climb steep, rocky slopes while hunting. I look for footholds that enable me to continue moving up and use them to my best advantage. Unfortunately, Satan does the same thing—using even seemingly small footholds to try to hinder our spiritual growth, raise doubt in our minds about God, and move us away from God's plan with lures that include money, power, fame, and sex.

With God's help, I strive to stay on the right path and not give the devil a foothold. I'm careful which movies I watch, for example, and which websites I visit. When bad patterns show up in my life, I discover the root (usually unmet needs) and seek to replace them—through God's power—with godly attitudes, speech, and actions. I'm still a 6' 4" work in progress, that's for sure.

I want to love people close to me well.

I don't want to end up in the bleachers; I want to be in the game!

I certainly don't want to be like that pronghorn buck that believed he was safe, yet ran right into a place of danger.

I don't want to become complacent and through inattention, ignorance, or predictability give Satan footholds in my life.

And I especially don't want to stray from God's truth and fall into Satan's traps. That doe followed the buck and paid the ultimate price.

I hope I'll remember that.

# 21

# It's Inevitable

I'd like to share a riddle with you.

> What always happens no matter who you are,
> Where you live,
> What your hobbies may be,
> Whether you are rich or poor, a veteran hunter or a
>    brand-new hunter,
> Whether you hunt with a rifle, bow, pistol, black-
>    powder rifle, or something else, and
> Whether you are happy or sad, purposeless or
>    purposeful?
> What always happens when you take action or don't
>    take action?
> When you desire things to happen—or not?
> And what is partly in your control, and yet may be
>    completely out of your control?

Figure it out?

It could be the wind starting to blow the wrong way as you stalk a deer, but I'm thinking of something different.

I'll give you a hint. It's a noun, verb, and synonym for loose coins in your pocket.

Did that help?

The answer is "change."

Change powerfully and constantly accompanies me during every hunting adventure. Consider the evolutions of my hunting gear.

My first firearm was a Marlin .22 rifle. Realizing that I could still hear well, I bought a louder shotgun and started pursuing game birds in addition to hunting small game such as rabbits. Then other weapons, including black-powder rifles and pistols, joined the mix.

My first cotton sleeping bag worked well until the outside temperature dropped below 50 degrees. Unfortunately, winter hunting temperatures often dipped well below that much of the time in our area, especially in our hunting tent. Tired of using up calories shivering at night instead of stalking during the day, I bought a down sleeping bag good down to -40 degrees F.

After my International two-wheel-drive truck couldn't make it up an icy hill during a raging snowstorm, I bought a '62 Willys Jeep. But its passenger door kept flying open and endangering people crazy enough to ride with me. When the turn-signal box on the steering-wheel column started smoking as I drove back from deer hunting, I cut off the wires in disgust and threw the box into the back—where it remained until I sold that vehicle. With no tears or regrets, I moved on to several Scout Travelers and then to my four-wheel-drive Ford F250 pickup.

And there's the evolution of sleeping accommodations too. Remember, I started big-game hunting later in years than some of you. The first several years I used an umbrella tent leftover from my teenage years. It was brutally holed on one side from an errant cherry-bomb firecracker and quite a sight during many hunting adventures. (Once several elk passed within 100 feet of my tent—probably to admire it. I was so touched by the scene I jerked the trigger and missed the shot.) When snow on top of my tent kept freezing and thawing, the roof leaked, so I wrapped it with a blue tarp that made it look—as one guy declared—"like a funny-looking blue ice cube." Since I had no heater during my early hunting years in below-zero winter conditions, he was more accurate than he knew!

The two buddies I usually hunted with and I managed to put cots, clothing, a table, cook stove, lantern, rifles, water jugs, and other items too numerous to mention into that tent simultaneously. Thinking about it now, I'm surprised the door zipper even closed. (I think Roy's military service in a submarine's close quarters made a huge difference.)

After 10-below nighttime temperatures for 5 days during another hunting trip, we chipped in and bought an old 24-foot fifth-wheel trailer for $2500. We still use it.

I guess I should comment on my first *tiny* hunting daypack, which might have been appropriate for a mountain man running for his life from an angry grizzly bear or an angry spouse waving an eight-pound, cast-iron fry pan. After never having enough room for snacks, water, ammo, and survival gear, I experimented with bigger packs. Now I use a military pack with many pockets and places to tie parachute cord. For shorter day hunts, I use a more compact pack.

My little closed-cell sitting pad—the thin, roll-up pad soldiers use—worked pretty well, but if I didn't scrape the ground well enough before putting it down, the sticks, pine cones, and rocks poked me. So, I started tying a plastic, fold-up camp seat to the back of my daypack. (Okay, maybe I am getting a little soft. But this has set me apart from macho hunters who sit for hours on sticks, pine cones, and sharp rocks.)

I've also experienced sleep-related changes. After hunting hard in rain, sleet, snow, sunshine, and wind, my hunting pals became afflicted with Snoring Disease. Night after night, I'd awaken to snorts, snores, mumbled words, and other noises you wouldn't want me to describe. It turns out I create such noises too, although I denied that profusely until a recorder nearly joined our gear pile. So I buy cheap silicone earplugs (my huge hearing protection earmuffs for shooting are too bulky to wear while sleeping on my side. Yes, I did really try to use them one night!). Not only do the silicone earplugs reduce the impact of Snoring Disease, they give me a weak excuse to disregard the four o'clock alarm for approximately six minutes. Then I force myself to get up to get hot water going on the stove for our oatmeal and coffee before predawn hunting expeditions.

My field-craft skills improved too. I learned to use a compass more accurately after hiking many extra miles in terrible conditions trying to return to our campsite. Anticipating that I might get turned around again, I eventually bought a better compass…and then a GPS unit (I still haven't entirely figured it out though).

Getting more to the "bottom" line…

After years of making do in mostly wilderness survival situations (surviving hunting camps in the early days took everything we could muster), I built an "outhouse" teepee out of three long, thin metal pieces and a blue tarp. I then made a porta-potty out of a five-gallon bucket and toilet seat. This evolution greatly improved our outlook on each new day, particularly during pelting snow, cuttingly cold north winds, and frozen ground that would have resisted a hand grenade, much less a shovel.

I could go on for 10 more pages at least outlining hunting changes I've experienced.

- Being almost forced at gunpoint to not cook dinner. Instead, we drove an hour each way to watch World Series games in restaurants that only offered overcooked burgers and fries and waitresses who called us "Honey."

- Beefing up first-aid supplies and tools in the futile attempt to address my experiences with cactus plants and old vehicles that break down.

- Delighting in not having to pump up the Coleman lantern gas tank because I now connect it to a propane bottle.

Life also provides an infinite number of changes—some wonderful, some good, some bad, some even worse.

- I can't carry a whole deer on my shoulders anymore. Sometimes I wish we had an ATV or a bodybuilding champion in camp to willingly carry any dead animals, such as elk, deer, and pronghorn, back to camp and not complain afterward.

- The average age of my hunting buddies and me is more than 70 years! (But don't call us old farts; we're still pretty sensitive.) Age equals more experience, right?

- I now have to wear gloves when it gets below 10 degrees.

- I need more padding underneath me when I sleep in my hunting tent because the ground keeps getting harder.

- I no longer apologize for requiring more than a powdered breakfast drink to keep me going until two in the afternoon. (I tell people I'm just getting smarter about nutrition. That makes me feel better about myself.)

Even Caitlin, my daughter, is getting older. During her younger days, she raised two 270-pound pigs while in 4-H. (We ate one and auctioned off the other one.) Talk about change! The timid girl who had a hard time guiding a headstrong pig in a 4-H ring is now a beautiful young woman who can afford to take Amanda and me out for thick pork chops. And she has job benefits I'll likely never have.

What types of changes have you experienced in hunting? In health? In finances? In your family? In friendships? In your community?

A more important question, and one I ask myself frequently, is "How well are you handling change?" Are you merely surviving? Thriving?

Sometimes I don't handle change well. Sometimes change hits me like a bullet striking a metal backstop. Because of these types of changes, I'm involved in the process of altering some of my thought patterns and emotional responses—with God's help and the help of wise family members and friends.

Right now my family and I are dealing with forest fire-related issues. The flames that chased me out of our home weeks ago (Amanda was out of state) burned most of our trees, our storage barn, our wood-splitter, and some of our dreams for the future. And now flash flooding is a major concern because rain runs down the scarred areas rather than soaking into the ground. We, like so many of our neighbors, are dealing with changes that force us to adjust.

Yet adjust we must.

Like the old-time merry-go-rounds that spin around a shaft, I need God at the center of my life. Sometimes life's changes make me dizzy or sick at heart. I can't get off the "Change Merry-Go-Round" or wave my hand like a magic wand and make everything stay the same. In terms of the forest fire, my burned trees now look like sticks and will never be alive again. The sap was literally boiled out of them.

If I could put the world on pause but be exempted, perhaps I'd take a few days to wander around to see what "no change" looks like. It would be my version of the film *Groundhog Day*, in which events in time keep repeating. Eventually I'd get so tired of the quiet—no wind blowing, no voices, no smiles directed at me, no ability to make root beer floats, no pistol shooting with friends, no geese flying across the sky in formation—that I'd hit the play button and reestablish change despite the difficulties it often brings.

I certainly don't want to remain the same way I was yesterday. I want to keep...

- growing spiritually, mentally, emotionally, and socially
- discovering more about God
- learning by facing and overcoming difficult issues
- nurturing and experiencing vibrant relationships
- trying new things to see what works and what doesn't

I'm sure you can relate.

A special friend of our family had a serious stroke. Every day in the hospital was a new day for her because, for many weeks, she couldn't remember what had happened the day before. Just imagine how confusing that was for her…and for those who loved her and visited her.

Fortunately God is at work in this crazy, ever-changing world. And I need his permanence. His unchanging nature. His endless power. His abiding love, and compassion, and forgiveness.

I'm glad he rejoices in hearing my prayers. Even ones like these: "Please, God, keep this truck running until we get over this mountain pass" or "Strengthen us so we can drag this beast another mile and up that steep hill."

He feels compassion when I still hurt from major surgery done years ago.

He comforts the pain in my heart when bad things happen to wonderful people I love.

He draws me toward the joyous promise of heaven.

He always keeps his promises: "The LORD is trustworthy in all he promises and faithful in all he does" (Psalm 145:13).

His revealed truths in the Scriptures remain constant and always true in a world where so many alleged truths collide.

He delights in you and me. "The LORD takes delight in his people" (Psalm 149:4).

He keeps giving this tired, sin-filled earth amazing sunsets. Funny-colored lizards. Beautiful but raucous peacocks. Gigantic elephants. Weird insects galore. Aspen leaves that spin in the wind. Areas without poison ivy or mosquitoes. Animal herds grazing in gorgeous meadows. And great hunting opportunities.

He sent his Son to us and for us. "God so loved the world that he gave his one and only Son, that whoever believes in him shall not perish but have eternal life" (John 3:16). "The Son is the image of the invisible God, the firstborn over all creation. For in him all things were created: things in heaven and on earth, visible and invisible" (Colossians 1:15-16).

Change is...and change will be. Many changes are beyond our complete understanding. I work hard day by day to invite God to always be the Rock on which I stand even as change happens.

Will you join me? Will you...

- rejoice when God answers change-related prayers?
- marvel as you watch a young child take his or her first steps?
- appreciate a smile from the thawing heart of a wounded spouse?
- thank God for the change-related lessons he teaches because he loves us?
- remember another change he offers? "Do not conform to the pattern of this world, but be transformed by the renewing of your mind" (Romans 12:2).

Think of the many personal change opportunities we're given every day. God doesn't want us to carry around the baggage of our sins. "If we confess our sins, [God] is faithful and just and will forgive us our sins and purify us from all unrighteousness" (1 John 1:9).

We can call on God no matter how discouraged, hopeless, or disgusted we feel. "Come to me, all you who are weary and burdened, and I will give you rest" (Matthew 11:28).

We can experience the living God of the universe. God tells us, "Be still, and know that I am God" (Psalm 46:10).

We can trust God to guide us through all the changes that life brings our way. "Trust in the LORD with all your heart and lean not on your own understanding; in all your ways submit to him, and he will make your paths straight. Do not be wise in your own eyes; fear the LORD and shun evil" (Proverbs 3:5-7).

During a break from writing this chapter, I talked with my wife as snow blew horizontally through our meadow. I was wondering how to end this chapter. Then it hit me. I experienced the greatest, most life-impacting change when I tackled this question: "Is God who he says he is?"

And after years of spiritual searching, I can declare, "*Yes!*"

I still know that's true.

# 22

# Living Life Expectantly

Animals and terrain often surprise me.

It happened again as my hunting buddies and I drove slowly down a dirt road about 2:30 one afternoon. We were looking for the distinctive outline of a buck pronghorn lying down or a small herd—any sign that it would be worthwhile to get out and start stalking. We frequently climbed out of the vehicle to study small hills and look into ravines where the light-colored pronghorn like to hang out.

After receiving permission from the ranch manager of this property, we'd carefully followed his instructions. "First go up that hill," he stated, pointing. "Then take the right fork and drive until you come to a Y. Go left, and once you pass under a ranch sign, go another mile until you come to a wire gate. You can hunt as soon as you go through that gate."

Even though we tried to hide our feelings of disappointment, the miles we'd already driven without seeing pronghorn weighed on each of us. *With gas prices so high,* I thought, *perhaps we were a bit crazy to think that driving even farther away from where we were staying would make much difference.*

Certainly our first day of hunting had been difficult—few animals sighted and no animals shot. The next day brought the same results. This wasn't the first time my buddies and I had experienced difficult hunting conditions, but not seeing pronghorn in Wyoming where there are more pronghorn than people confounded us. *Where are the pronghorn?* I kept asking myself. Herds of animals usually crisscrossed this entire region. A fish and game biologist told me that more than 55,000 pronghorn usually stayed in this area. My hunting buddies and I had looked forward to these days for nearly a year, and now our time was passing by much too quickly.

We felt privileged to be on this private land because the ranch manager admitted that he was fed up with hunters who disobeyed ranch rules or didn't care to learn about them in the first place. "One hunter," he told me privately, "shot a pronghorn near that building over there a week ago without permission when we weren't home."

Clearly this was ideal pronghorn habitat. Several small reservoirs a few miles apart contained water, though levels were low. Short grass covered the fields, and well-positioned pronghorn could see predators a long way off. All of this, plus the three of us being the only hunters in this area, should have encouraged us and resulted in many sightings.

We kept rolling down the Jeep's windows to glass terrain. Frequently we parked and headed out in different directions, still believing that pronghorn might be over the next hill standing in tall sagebrush or lying down near a snow fence or knoll.

We kept calculating wind as we checked out ravines and shadowed areas out on the plain, as well as tiny gullies. Stopping short of the crest of each hill, we'd creep up and over time after time, hour after hour. Believing that any second we'd see pronghorn.

After several more miles of driving and stopping, we drove over a small hill and came to a gate about 30 yards in front of us. "Well," Walt said, "I guess this is as far as we can go. There aren't any animals in here anyway."

Just as he said that, four pronghorn—a buck and three does—dashed right in front of the Jeep about 20 feet away! The three of us watched in amazement as they disappeared, leaving a small cloud of dust in their wake. We never even had time to get out of our vehicle!

If we'd slowly peeked over the top of this last hill as we'd done for all those previous hills instead if just driving over it, we might have seen those animals sooner and been able to shoot.

It's easy to second-guess hunting strategies during times like this, but such criticism usually makes the situation worse. I didn't do that this time fortunately. Without talking about it, we all knew we'd overlooked a critically important aspect of our hunt. We'd allowed ourselves to become complacent instead of being filled with anticipation at what the next 100 yards—or even the next 20 feet—might bring.

We'd not been hunting expectantly.

I see parallels between this experience and my life. I sometimes find myself focusing so intently on what I see or don't see happening that I live as if what's going on right this moment is all there is. I lose sight of the future blessings God promises I'll enjoy.

I overlook that God's plans for this world are in motion.

I forget that he has plans for me each day.

I lose sight of living expectantly, especially when difficulties sap my strength, cause pain in my heart, and erase hope from my mind.

Does this happen to you too? Difficulties are like water leaking from a roof into a living room and splashing into a bucket. We want them to go away now, but they don't until we deal with them.

We all face difficulties. Disappointments. Debilitating physical injuries. Agony while watching loved ones suffer. Pain when our children choose harmful—even deadly—paths. Financial struggles. Sexual temptations. Addiction issues. Protective attitudes. Selfish actions. Fear. Self-doubt. Depression. Insecurities.

Which difficulties make your Top 10 list of rotten things? I find it all too easy to focus on myself...

- rather than on God and what he desires to teach me through difficulties.

- rather than on people who need me to stand firm through God's power and come alongside them in love.

- rather than living expectantly, believing and being excited about what God is doing in and through me and other Christ followers no matter how difficult the situations may be.

It's easy for me to look behind and down rather than ahead and up, focusing my heart and mind on God and his plans. Thankfully, when I so easily forgot the most positive, joy-filled, peace-giving, "wow is this great truth," God reminds me gently.

This happened one evening when I was discussing spiritual living with a few followers of Jesus. A friend named Russ asked, "So what difference do you think heaven makes in our lives today?"

That struck a cynical chord in me. "I don't think about heaven," I stated. "I'm too busy dealing with life right now. When I get there, I get there."

Sadness crossed Russ's face. "I find great comfort," he said slowly, "in thinking about heaven. It makes a lot of difference to me right now."

Have you ever experienced a time when heartfelt, truth-filled words nearly knocked you off your chair? Shot through all your defenses? Penetrated your heart and mind? May even have caused a sense of sadness and loss to well up inside you? That happened to me at that moment.

Russ was right.

I'd allowed life's difficulties and the emotional pain I'd buried inside to harden my heart and steal the joy, peace, and other special things God desired to give me. I'd become a weary life traveler shuffling down a dusty road on a hot day. A guy who had forgotten the truth that God's Living Water was within my grasp, ready to quench my spiritual thirst and refocus my priorities. I hadn't learned to live life expectantly in light of God's character and promises…and especially in light of spending eternity with him in heaven.

I'd held on to my pain rather than facing it and working through it.

I'd never allowed myself to focus my mind *and* my heart on the joy and freedom that comes from experiencing the power of the resurrected Jesus, who intercedes for me.

I'd disregarded the hope of once again spending time with loved ones who were already rejoicing in heaven.

I hadn't pondered my future life in God's eternal kingdom, where Christ followers will never again experience pain, or tears, or confusion, or disappointment, or unmet emotional needs. Where joy will fill every heart.

After the truth in Russ's words broke into my heart, a little of my self-protective hardness melted. "Really?" I felt like shouting. "How do I live that way? I'm tired and beaten down, struggling to provide for my family, wrestling with feelings of insecurity, fed up with physical pain that drains me, feeling angry that life isn't easy. After all, I'm trying to serve God, and shouldn't that make life much easier?"

Check out these verses that powerfully address the hope that each of us can have because of what's coming:

> Praise be to the God and Father of our Lord Jesus Christ! In his great mercy he has given us new birth into a living hope through the resurrection of Jesus Christ from the dead, and into an inheritance that can never perish, spoil or fade. This inheritance is kept in heaven for you, who through faith are shielded by God's power until the coming of the salvation that is ready to be revealed in the last time. In all this you greatly rejoice, though now for a little while you may have had to suffer grief in all kinds of trials. These have come so that the proven genuineness of your faith—of greater worth than gold, which perishes even though refined by fire—may result in praise, glory and honor when Jesus Christ is revealed (1 Peter 1:3-7).

> You ought to live holy and godly lives as *you look forward to* the day of God and speed its coming (2 Peter 3:11-12).

Amazingly, everything happening on earth right now pales in comparison to what's ahead for each of us who has a personal relationship with God through Jesus! The apostle Paul, knowing how easy it is for people to focus on this life without living expectantly with heaven in mind, wrote that our real citizenship "is in heaven." We are to "eagerly await" Jesus, who "will transform our lowly bodies so that they will be like his glorious body" (Philippians 3:20-21).

These days I'm learning—moment by moment, hour by hour, day by day—to trust God, expectantly looking for the great visible or invisible things he will accomplish in and through me. In God's economy nothing is wasted! He even uses my weaknesses, doubts, hurts from emotional wounds, fear, and sadness to draw me closer to him and be able to relate to people who also face similar things.

God desires to partner with you and me to accomplish wonderful things within our respective spheres of influence. No matter what's happened in our past, a new and bright future awaits us. Heaven is our pot of gold at the end of the rainbow.

I'm starting to joyfully anticipate eternity in heaven—almost as much as I anticipate my next hunting trip. That's a change, for sure. I want to—I *choose* to—live expectantly, believing there's a pronghorn waiting for me just over the next rise.

# 23

# Camouflage

Certainly hunters have used camouflage since the earliest times. They've hidden in tall grass, up in trees, and behind rocks and brush in ravines. To get closer to animals, people have worn animal skins and walked "on four legs"—bent over with arms dangling. They've waited strategically at selected watering holes. Crawled long distances. Spent hours in treestands. Sat under trees in deep snow. All with the objective of getting within the kill range of bows, spears, blowguns, slings, knives, rocks, muzzleloaders, air-powered guns, longbows, crossbows, high-powered rifles, shotguns, pistols, and countless other weapons.

Just as our hunting gear has greatly improved in efficiency, camouflage has come a long way too. Now it's tailored for such locations as light-colored forests, open plains, snow-covered slopes, and dense timber. The science of blending in to one's surroundings is big business now. We buy camouflaged everything, including boots, coats, hats, gloves, face veils and masks, vests, T-shirts, sitting pads, netting, dog-training devices, and treestands.

And let's not forget insulated camo clothing with the latest and greatest waterproof, breathable, you-name-it option allowing us to hike miles in comfort even in awful weather. Also lightweight ghillie suits making us look like hairy, twiggy beasts, and outfits with a ton of fake leaves to help us resemble walking trees, albeit with no branches or squirrels. One of my turkey-hunting friends tries to look like parts of a tree. Except for his eyes, he succeeds, and turkeys have walked right up to him—and never strutted away.

Smart manufacturing folks help us hide things we didn't even know needed to be hidden. According to recent catalogs, camo chaise lounges will make me less conspicuous as I drink a soda. Insulated kennel jackets will hide my dog. Blind covers will help geese remain content while I hold my breath and watch them fly in. Camo rifle stocks will help conceal my black-powder rifles, especially if I lean one against a tree. Camo seat covers will make my rear less conspicuous while I'm driving across a field toward a great hunting area.

I've even seen a photograph of a camo comforter and shams for my bed in case, I'm assuming, the huge buck I'm hunting the next morning peeks into my window to figure out when I'll start hunting. I wouldn't want him to know my intentions, right? Maybe on a "cold but still great weather" day for hunting I could just cut a hole out of the center of that comforter, slip it on with my head sticking out, make several additional holes for my arms, and I'd remain warm and comfy in a little hollow.

Military organizations around the world keep coming up with new camo patterns that are usually computer generated. I saw a navy uniform a while back that would definitely keep any sailor who fell overboard from being seen by rescue personnel.

In order to introduce a bit more of a solid color into the hunting mix where I live, Colorado wildlife folks publish wildlife regulations spelling out what hunters must wear in the field while hunting specific species and during certain dates. I can wear camo while bow hunting in September, but when I rifle hunt for deer or elk I must wear a fluorescent orange hat and outer orange vest that together make up 500 square inches. Wearing orange isn't up for debate in Colorado, and I always feel silly wearing it.

Are big-game animals and game birds color-blind? Do at least some of them recognize orange and relate it to being worn during certain times of the year by dangerous critters who want to kill them? Orange isn't exactly a nature color (except on deciduous trees in the fall). According to a Missouri Department of Conservation site, research done by the University of Georgia "proved that deer are red–green color-blind." Yes, I googled the words "deer recognizing orange" and discovered that. Perhaps I could do the same type of search for each species I hunt. Then I could see if anybody breaks down his or her summary conclusions about orange according to the position of the moon, the hunting month, weather factors, and other parameters. Most likely I'll never know the definitive answer for each species. If you compile a list, please send it to me (along with your sources).

Since I don't have a large hunting budget, I typically wear military-surplus camo pants with many button-down pockets (the ones with Velcro make too much noise), dark-colored shirts, and earth-toned jackets and coats that don't reflect light and have no white on them. (White is an alarm signal for many animals.) I also have camo gloves and other accessories. My choices, like yours, are obviously guided by what I'm hunting and weather conditions.

I still have a few camo-related questions though.

Can predators such as coyotes, big-game animals such as elk, and game birds such as turkeys make laughing sounds when certain types of camo don't work? Or do attentive animals, birds, and waterfowl just run or fly away?

What do these same creatures think when a portable camo blind suddenly shows up on opening day? Or camouflaged humans suddenly start wearing hunter orange only when entering or leaving a forest?

During one October elk hunt, I wore my typical earth-colored clothing and hiked a mile or so to a series of long meadows shortly before sunrise. I'd walked through this area a few days earlier and chosen a central spot in which to sit. It still seemed perfect—behind a fir tree at the edge of dark timber. I cleared away sticks and leaves in the immediate vicinity so I could shift positions quietly, and I moved some tree branches that were in my field of vision. The wind was blowing toward me, carrying my scent away from the meadow.

Within a few minutes, I blended in pretty well, but I'm sure my outfit didn't make me look like a tall, skinny tree wearing an orange hat. (Hmm, maybe I need to rethink my gear—again.)

For the next two hours, I sat there blending in with my surroundings. I listened to squirrels, heard the wing beats of large birds overhead, watched a chipmunk dig in leaves, and tried to keep warmth in and cold out. Sometimes I dozed for 15 or 20 seconds at a time, but I'm sure I kept my mouth closed so my white teeth wouldn't show. Okay, maybe I dozed in 45-second intervals.

As I scanned the meadows for perhaps the fiftieth time, I got one of the most positive shocks of my life! A large cow elk and her teenaged calf had entered the meadow to my left, about 150 yards away. *Where were they hiding?* I wondered. Warily, the cow took a few steps, pausing to sniff the air and look around. Detecting no danger, she entered the meadow. Slowly and deliberately I stopped pretending I was a tree, shifted my position slightly, raised my rifle, aimed, and shot. She took one more step and then dropped to the ground.

She never saw me. My clothing selection had worked. Her calf, large enough to fend for itself, bellowed for a while and then moved into the timber.

After attaching my signed and dated carcass tag to the cow's ear, I field dressed the animal and went to locate friends or strangers who would help me drag the beast to the nearest road. There was no hiding my joy. I kept thinking, *I'm so lucky to be here hunting elk. And I actually got one!* I thought about how well my somewhat camouflaged clothing had worked this time.

But what about when I'm not hunting? Unfortunately, I realized that when a particular hunting season is over I'm challenged by other issues of camouflage—specifically the ways I try to hide parts of myself when I'm with other people.

No, I don't wear camo pants to an important meeting or a camo mask when I'm invited to stop by a party where I don't know anybody. I don't lie in a park in a ghillie suit to see if a dog will run up to me and mark his territory on my synthetic strings.

Sometimes, though, I find myself trying to hide my weaknesses—worries about finances, oversensitivity to criticism, cravings for alcohol when I'm really stressed (I quit drinking more than 30 years ago), insecurities regarding self-worth, envy when somebody drives by in a new pickup truck, and the fear of being fully known by people who might use that knowledge to hurt me.

It's risky to let people see the real me.

The guy who sometimes wrestles with sexual temptations.

The guy who feels his prayers bounce off the ceiling occasionally.

The guy who is content to have only one suit to wear for weddings and funerals (even when I get dirty looks from the more fashion conscious).

I hide who I am, erecting invisible, self-protective walls by...

- not sharing what I'm feeling or thinking with guys in a small group at church.
- not being open about a sin I keep repeating.
- trying to keep deep wounds covered up and hidden from even my wife and closest friends.
- not trusting God 24/7 to handle my most difficult issues and those of other people.
- pushing shattered dreams into a corner of my heart instead of grieving and allowing healing to flow into me from God and his people.
- getting down on myself instead of using laughter to help me cope sometimes, such as when I cut a board a quarter inch too short or forget how to tie a necktie.

Fortunately, through God's grace and the wisdom and love of Christ followers who encourage me by word and example and accept me as I am, in recent years especially I've been reaping the joys of dropping my personal camouflage and being more transparent as I stand firmly for Jesus in ways I never did before.

It's not easy.

I don't want people to see me miss an easy shot in the field, forget to take my gun off safety when I'm ready to shoot, or rip my pants on a barbed-wire fence.

I don't want people to see that I can no longer put a deer around my neck and carry it a mile or more in rough terrain.

To help me stay far away from personal camouflage, I'm learning to rely on God more and to truly believe that he loves me just the way I am. He cares more about my *being* than he does about my *doing*. He sees right through my efforts at personal camouflage and lovingly touches my wounded heart and mind. He reinforces that he created me with certain strengths and corresponding weaknesses so that I need him and other Christ followers to keep growing spiritually as a disciple of Jesus.

The illusion that I'm safer when I use personal camouflage to hide my insecurities, weaknesses, and failures from God and other people is a lie from our spiritual enemy, Satan. This adversary hates it when godly men (and women) strive to love God and people and desire to develop godly character that reflects Jesus even when no one is watching.

I'm thankful that God gives me courage, hope, and enthusiasm during my Bible and prayer times.

I'm grateful for the new freedom I experience as God helps me drop self-protective camo in my prayers, in relating to my wife and daughter, in my discussions with other people.

When I've buried sinful or painful things almost too deep to find, my wise family members and friends help me to acknowledge and face them. These people remind me that the light of God's forgiveness and his healing power shrivel up bad things just like exposed maggots die in the hot sun or are eaten by birds.

Maybe you also use personal camouflage to hide parts of who you really are—what you really believe, your deepest desires and goals, your struggles and wrongdoings. If so, join the party! I even have candles and matches, but I don't know what kind of cake you prefer. Remember, no matter what types of camouflage you use, you're not alone.

Using camouflage is a normal response. Not using it can be an arduous, uphill climb and is often countercultural. Personal camouflage even flourishes within some churches and youth groups. When Adam and Eve hid behind fig leaves in the Garden of Eden after they sinned, they were *afraid*! Fear is the first emotion mentioned in the Bible after God expressed pleasure in all of his creation.

Wisdom Jesus shared with his disciples still applies to those of us who follow him today:

> You are the light of the world. A town built on a hill cannot be hidden. Neither do people light a lamp and put it under a bowl. Instead they put it on its stand, and it gives light to everyone in the house. In the same way, let your light shine before others, that they may see your good deeds and glorify your Father in heaven (Matthew 5:14-16).

If you see me wearing a camo mask sometime, whether it's visible or invisible, please ask me how I'm doing, okay? Ask in love. With sincerity. Because you really want to know.

There's no freedom in living behind a mask and breathing old, unhealthy, recycled air.

# The "One in Seven" Strategy

When I first started hunting the *Antilocapra Americana*—the "American antelope goat," aka "pronghorn"—I didn't know what a unique and remarkable animal it is. Scientists consider it to be the sole surviving member of a family of ungulates (hoofed animals) dating back millions of years.

Pronghorn have branched horns and shed them each year. They are the fastest land animal in the Western hemisphere. (If I'd known this, I might have been even more intimidated by the prospect of hunting them.) A pronghorn is very curious and has excellent eyesight and depth perception. It can spot slight movements up to four miles away. This animal lives in prairie and desert habitats with temperatures ranging between 130 degrees and -50 degrees F.

Two years ago, I decided to try a new technique for pronghorn hunting. Since wildlife regulations where I hunt require hunters to shoot away from highways, a certain distance from highways, and on the other side of easement boundary fencing, I used to try to cross over the fences unnoticed by my eagle-eyed prey. Unfortunately, leaning a rifle against a fence and then either rolling under a fence or climbing over it without catching my coat or pants on barbed wire are not subtle, hidden activities.

You can guess what happened next.

Mostly what I gained from my efforts were views of the hind-quarters of vanishing pronghorn and souvenirs of cactus spines in my knees and elbows.

When my friends and I tried to do complicated stalks ("you go way around behind that far hill, and I'll sneak over the fence and down that dried-up creek bed…"), we usually wasted at least an hour of hunting time getting into position, and we never could get close enough to take effective shots.

After a particularly long stalk went badly and it took us more than two hours to regroup, I talked with my buddies about breaking out of the normal ways of thinking and strategizing. Since prong-horn have binocular vision, I considered a new approach I call the "One in Seven" technique.

It's not hard to apply.

It doesn't require great fence-crossing abilities.

It takes far less time to implement—usually 10 minutes or less—than most other strategies.

After spotting pronghorn between 150 and 300 yards away, I walk nonchalantly up to the fence as if I'm thinking about pizza. I lean my rifle against a sturdy post and take my time climbing over, pretending I don't care that pronghorn are nearby.

Figuring the animals read body language, I avoid looking at them and project an attitude that communicates "Hey, even though I see you, I really don't care that you're there. I'm just out here to enjoy the scenery. And climbing over fences is great exercise."

After I've crossed the fence, and only then, do I figure out how far away the pronghorn have moved after first spotting me. The first time I did this, they'd moved about 500 yards. At least they were still in the county.

I kept trying the "One in Seven" strategy.

You know what I discovered? The first six times I applied it, the pronghorn ran up to 55 miles an hour and stopped up to 750 or so yards away. But the *seventh* time (and I know that I'm stretching personification license, but stay with me), the pronghorn seemed to think, "Hey, that 6' 4" guy with big feet has no idea that we can see him so well and run away so fast. I wonder what he's thinking as we stand here 300 yards away. Is he admiring our good looks and our ability to thrive in this challenging terrain?" (I won't go so far as to speculate that they were planning to walk up to me and welcome me to their turf. That would be presumptuous.)

Anyway, I kept a large power-line pole between the pronghorn and me. From about 200 yards, I shot and killed a pronghorn.

This brings to mind another hunting adventure that started out as a "One in Seven." It's etched in my memory as one of my favorite stalks ever. I climbed over the four-wire fence as if I had all the time in the world. I looked around the huge pasture, pretending I was hunting for the petrified wood that's all around the area I was in. All the while I kept walking toward a group of five pronghorn as they milled around. The large buck recognized danger sooner than his four does and guided his harem to an open area 600 yards away from me.

Rather than following them, I headed west, walking slowly toward where I'd seen 35 or so pronghorn earlier as we drove by on the main highway. The crisp October air was refreshing as I kept my eyes on the horizon, hoping to see a pronghorn before it saw me.

Avoiding the sagebrush, I walked a mile or so. Suddenly I saw a pronghorn head through the top of a grassy clump…and then another! I hunched over to where I could no longer see them and kept walking. After moving 100 yards farther, I had to take off my pack and drop to a prone position in order to keep seeing only their heads through the grass.

Boy was I excited! I reminded myself to crawl slowly and be as relaxed as possible. No way was I going to mess up this stalk. Five minutes later, I clearly saw a large doe standing on my side of a small hill. I focused on her. Hesitant to move much closer in case she'd see me, I crawled just a little bit more. I kept studying her through my scope (at six power). She was eating, her left side facing me.

I placed my portable bipod on the barrel of my .243, aimed up from her lungs but below her back behind her front leg, and squeezed the trigger.

Immediately heads popped up all over. Animals ran in every direction, including the doe I'd shot at.

*Did I miss?* I wondered, standing up. Four pronghorn still didn't want to leave their sheltered area, but I knew the importance of see-ing what had happened to the first animal before shooting at another one. When I reached the spot where the doe had been standing, I saw no blood…and no pronghorn. I started walking north around the hill, and there she was.

I felt several emotions as I looked down at her dead body. Cer-tainly I was elated. My strategy had worked well! I had stalked effec-tively and placed my bullet well. I also found myself thinking about the pronghorn's beauty, skill, and freedom to run the hills and plains. I think if I had the opportunity to be a wild animal, being a prong-horn would be at the top of my list. I reminded myself of what a wildlife officer had told me as I researched this hunting area. "We're thankful for hunters like you who reduce the population." Hunting is necessary for conservation and good resource management.

I felt better.

I reached down and unzipped my backpack. I pulled out my sharp Buck knife, a quart of water, some paper towels, and a plastic bag for the liver. (Yes, I'm one of those guys who loves liver, bacon, and onions—at least the way my wife cooks them!). Then I field dressed the doe. Twenty minutes later, my buddies spotted me in the field and came over to my location. We placed the doe in the back on two tarps and headed back to camp to hang her on a homemade rack out of the sun. I didn't skin her right away because dry winds can harden exposed meat to shoe-leather consistency.

Reflecting on that time, I'm still touched by how perfectly God created the pronghorn and how easily I get caught up in the daily grind and overlook his creativity. The Bible says, "Since the creation of the world God's invisible qualities—his eternal power and divine nature—have been clearly seen, being understood from what has been made" (Romans 1:20). As I ponder the pronghorn's oversized lungs and windpipe, strong heart, hollow hair that helps to resist cold, and light bones for speed while running, I'm in awe of how God arranged so many details perfectly.

When hunting season ends and I see pronghorn, I often pull off the road to observe them and marvel at their uniqueness. Deep inside I envy them a little bit. After all, they get to run at high speeds and observe the world with their keen vision. What a way to experience life!

I hope I'll always remember my hunting adventures, but even more I hope I develop a keener thankfulness toward the God who made all this possible.

Oh, and if you try the "One in Seven" approach and get caught on a barbed-wire fence, please don't send me a photo. Certain things are best left to the imagination or forgotten entirely.

# Thankfulness

For years I've stepped purposefully on various paths while hunting. I've walked along railroad tracks, through cornfields, up steep mountain trails, across huge pastures leased to ranchers for cattle grazing, down game trails during snowstorms, in very wet places, around rocky slopes…Some paths are easy to navigate; some paths are difficult and dangerous. Reflecting on these paths, I find myself thinking about the people who have guided me down the "hunting path." Some of them never even knew it!

A camp counselor whose name I don't remember encouraged me when I was a skinny teenager to pick up a .22 rifle at a little rifle range and practice enough to earn a Junior NRA Sharpshooter award. (I still have that treasured pin in a special box!)

A year or so after that, a guy named Jerry taught me backcountry skills and tempered my youthful enthusiasm with common sense and compassion. Once when I chased a porcupine about 30 feet up a pine tree, Jerry stated dryly, "What'll happen if he falls on your head after you poke him with that stick?"

Gary, a high school friend, joined me during winter finger-freezing pheasant and rabbit hunts. (If you read this, Gary, please call me!) Through him, I learned more about the value of quality companionship.

In his fifties, my father-in-law began accompanying me on what sometimes turned out to be less like hunting trips and more like *survival* excursions. And Roy guided me down the most important path of all—spiritual growth as a disciple of Jesus.

Walt, my longtime hunting buddy, gently taught me a great deal about friendship, influence, making a difference for the kingdom of God, and hunting strategies he learned as a child growing up in Africa.

My wife, Amanda, who for years has prepared great hunting camp meals, has hunted with me on various occasions, and has spent hours cutting up and packaging game meat. She also juggles household responsibilities so I can take extended hunting trips.

To this list, I could add kind landowners, cooperative wildlife officers, and a neighbor named Jeff who, for many years, loaned me great equipment for sighting in my rifles. I'm thankful for these people and others too numerous to mention because they've all had a hand in guiding me along the paths of life.

Who comes to mind when you think about the special people in your life? Who helped you walk around the next bend when you felt lost? Who stood by you through all sorts of adventures and misadventures? Who reminded you to stay focused on God?

I'm also learning to be more aware of evidences of God's handiwork and blessings so I can appreciate them and thank him. Brilliant orange sunsets. Warm rays of sun breaking through the trees as another hunting day unfolds. Unexpected finds at thrift stores, such as a canvas wall tent and a propane lantern. A gift from a friend—a winch that removes most of the pain of loading large, dead animals into my pickup truck. A newborn fawn trying to remain unseen in tall grass. A majestic bull elk guiding his herd into dark timber at first light. The ability to climb a steep hill and observe deer browsing in a meadow. Steaming deer pellets that indicate that the huge buck I'm tracking may be just around the next bend.

Which blessings and hunting experiences bring a smile to your face and create thankfulness in your heart?

The apostle Paul, an incredible traveler who faced hardships few of us will ever face, recognized the importance of thankfulness: "So then, just as you received Christ Jesus as Lord, continue to live your lives in him, rooted and built up in him, strengthened in the faith as you were taught, and overflowing with thankfulness" (Colossians 2:6-7). A little later Paul reinforced his point: "Be thankful" (3:15).

By the way, are you a *cultivator*?

I'm not talking about a guy driving a tractor in a field.

Or someone who tills a garden plot, uses strings and stakes to mark where seeds go, and nurtures those seeds.

Or someone who over time develops skills such as reloading ammo, choosing the right site for a blind, tracking a wounded animal, or building a snow cave during a blizzard.

I'm talking about being a different kind of *cultivator*—being a person who encourages, provides knowledge and wisdom, and expresses thankfulness to those who have blessed you during your hunting endeavors and daily life:

- the checkout woman who smiles kindly and makes it easier for you to patiently wait when the person in front of you decides not to buy three items she's already paid for…and you're anxious to buy the two items you forgot to pack and get hunting

- the buddy who tells you to observe the shifting clouds and approaching snow and evaluate how it will impact your hunting experiences

- the friend who lets you borrow a rifle every year…and helps you process the meat you bring home

- the spouse who respects you and eagerly loves you before and after your hunting trips—whether you bring home meat or not and no matter how dirty your hunting clothes may be

- the special person who helps you process life's tough issues while sitting by a campfire…or at least tries to get you to talk about them so you know you don't have to handle them on your own

I want to leave you with two important questions I often ask myself: How might your life be different if you express sincere thankfulness to God and to people at least five times a day? What if you put as much energy into being thankful as you put into planning and carrying out hunting strategies?

Speaking of thankfulness, I'm grateful to you for taking the time to read these stories. I hope they encouraged your walk in Jesus, strengthened your faith in God, and increased your enthusiasm for hunting.

Thank you.

## About the Author

An enthusiastic outdoorsman, **Stephen W. Sorenson** is an award-winning writer and editor, guest speaker, and volunteer chaplain. In addition to operating Sorenson Communications, he and his wife, Amanda, enjoy outdoor activities with family and friends, including hunting, camping, hiking, fishing, and traveling. Stephen is also an avid harmonica player. The Sorensons live in Colorado.

If you'd like Stephen to speak to your group about hunting, discovering God in everyday life, or other topics, please contact him at stephenspeaks@gmail.com.

If you enjoyed
***I'd Rather Be Hunting,***
you'll also like these bestselling books
by Steve Chapman

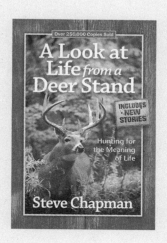

## A Look at Life from a Deer Stand

From the incredible rush of bagging "the big one" to standing in awe of God's magnificent creation, Steve Chapman captures the spirit of the hunt. In short chapters filled with excitement and humor, he takes you on his successful and not-so-successful forays into the heart of deer country. As you experience the joy of scouting a trophy buck or getting a large doe, you'll discover how the skills necessary for great hunting can help you draw closer to the Lord.

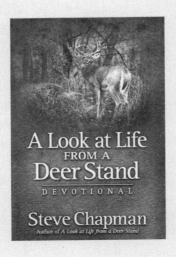

## A Look at Life from a Deer Stand Devotional

Just you, God, and a whitetail. Perfect. From the moment he hits the woods to the minute he heads home, avid hunter Steve Chapman revels in the pursuit of whitetails. A vivid storyteller, he invites you to join him in the thickets, meadows, and woods to experience God's magnificent creation and discover powerful truths that reveal the awesome ways He guides you.

From the pulse-racing sight of a trophy buck to insights gleaned from a wily doe, these enthusiastic devotions will add to your hunting knowledge as you celebrate God's presence and provision.

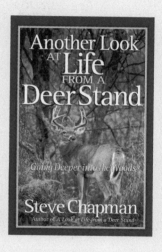

## Another Look at Life from a Deer Stand

Drawing on his many years of hunting, avid sportsman Steve takes you to the forests and fields to experience the excitement of sighting whitetails and wily turkeys. From the joys of being the woods to the thrill of handling well-made equipment, you'll relate to the adventure of going after wild game. Along the way you'll also garner some intriguing life truths that will impact your everyday life...spiritual truths that reflect the bounty and grace of the Creator.

To learn more about Harvest House books and
to read sample chapters, visit our website:

**www.harvesthousepublishers.com**

HARVEST HOUSE PUBLISHERS
EUGENE, OREGON